ORIENTEERING MADE SIMPLE AN INSTRUCTIONAL HANDBOOK

By

Nancy Kelly

ISBN: 1-4140-0893-7 (e-book)
ISBN: 1-4140-0892-9 (Paperback)

This book is printed on acid free paper.

1stBooks - rev.08/09/06

TABLE OF CONTENTS

SECTION ONE
INDOOR MAP SKILLS

SECTION TWO
OUTDOOR MAP SKILLS

SECTION THREE
USING A COMPASS

MAP ADVENTURE PROGRAMS

Orienteering is a sport that is all about maps. It can be enjoyed by people of all ages, either as a recreational activity or as a competitive sport. This book is designed to introduce orienteering to school students as well as youth organizations of all ages.

MULTIDISCIPLINARY APPROACH

In a carefully designed step-by-step process, participants learn to navigate first in a classroom, then in a schoolyard or park, and finally in the forest at a regular orienteering meet. The entire process is one that fosters:

SELF CONFIDENCE	**COOPERATIVE LEARNING**
PROBLEM SOLVING	TEAM BUILDING
DECISION-MAKING	**LOVE FOR THE OUTDOORS**

Programs are easily adaptable to a wide variety of grade levels and can be designed to enhance most subject areas. Below is a sampling of concepts and skills that can be experienced through orienteering and orienteering maps.

PERSONAL DEVELOPMENT
Self-esteem
Problem Solving
Self-confidence
Team building
Organizational skills
Responsibility
Concentration
Social relationships
Memory skills
Decision making

MATH
Estimating
Work problems
Mental computation
Calculating
Metric system
Real life applications
Pacing
Spatial relationships
Precision

SCIENCE
magnetism
contour interpretation
land forms
habitat analysis
ecology
compass usage

LANGUAGE ARTS
writing about experiences
listening
Comprehension
writing directions

PHYSICAL EDUCATION
aerobic activity
lifetime sports
skill assessment
cooperative learning
personal health

SOCIAL STUDIES
exploring
new environments
map legends
handling skills
grids
land usage

ART
observation
drawing
perspective
visualization

TECHNOLOGY
surveying
computer drawing
photogrammetry
internet communications
software applications

TYPES OF ORIENTEERING

Orienteering courses can be set in any environment where an appropriate map has been made.

STRING ORIENTEERING: Used with preschoolers and primary grade children. Controls are placed along a string, which leads the child to each of the control.

STAR ORIENTEERING: Participants must return to start between each control. Used mainly for training.

MOTALA (individual or group relay): Excellent for schoolyards and small areas. Participants do a loop of several controls and return to the start.

TRIVIA ORIENTEERING: Proof of arrival at each control site is confirmed by answering a question about the site.

MYSTERY ORIENTEERING: Maps are marked indicating controls to be located. Participants mark off clues on their scorecard when they find the control with the clue on it. This is an excellent training event for improving map-reading skills.

LINE ORIENTEERING: Maps are marked with a line indicating the exact route to be followed. Participants mark their map where they find each control. Good for beginner map reading skill training.

PROJECT ORIENTEERING: At each control the participant attempts to complete some type of activity. The activity may be used to teach a new concept or used to test a skill.

CROSS COUNTRY (point to point): A course of controls to be taken in a specific order is laid out. Lengths vary from a few kilometers for beginners to ten or more kilometers for experts. Classic form of orienteering.

SCORE ORIENTEERING: Participants try to find as many controls as possible in a given amount of time. Controls usually have different point values depending upon distance from the start and the difficulty of control placement.

Other types of orienteering are:

- Bike orienteering
- Canoe orienteering
- Ski orienteering
- Trail orienteering- designed for those with disabilities

MULTIDISCIPLINARY TECHNIQUES TAUGHT THROUGH MAP ADVENTURES

COURSE DESCRIPTION

Orienteering is a lifetime activity in which the participant uses a detailed map to develop strategies on how to navigate to a series of locations. Orienteering is both a competitive and recreational sport with a number of concepts and skills that can easily be integrated into the classroom. Through adaptations of orienteering, students can explore new areas of learning in many different subject areas. This exciting addition to any curriculum can be modified for preschool through college age. The skills of orienteering also apply to everyday navigation with a variety of maps. Orienteering is an excellent vehicle for developing problem solving, decision- making, cooperative learning, and improving self-esteem.

COURSE OUTLINE

Goals: Through a series of hands-on activities, participants will learn about orienteering and explore the many ways orienteering can be incorporated into their school programs using a multidisciplinary teaching approach.

Objectives:

1. The learner will become familiar with orienteering as a sport and teaching technique.
2. The learner will identify the types of orienteering.
3. The learner will develop basic orienteering techniques.
4. The learner will use these techniques to teach orienteering.
5. The learner will develop activities to incorporate orienteering into his/her current school program.
6. The learner will be introduced to orienteering materials and resources.
7. The learner will learn how to make simple orienteering maps.
8. The learner will design and set up an orienteering course.
9. The learner will explore way orienteering can be used to develop self-confidences and decision-making.
10. The learner will discover ways orienteering can be used as a cooperative learning activity.
11. The learner will develop navigational and map handling skills.
12. The learner will have opportunities to enhance problem-solving skills.

SECTION ONE

FIRST STEPS IN ORIENTEERING
INDOOR MAP SKILLS

INTRODUCTION TO ORIENTEERING

THE EVENT

In orienteering participants receive a map of an area that shows a series of sites. Participants develop strategies, which they use to navigate to locate these sites. It is a sport that can be done both competitively and for fun. It blends both mental and physical activity. It is often referred to as **THE THINKING SPORT** or **CUNNING RUNNING**.

Orienteering can begin in a small area like a classroom and everything in the room is very specific; example, top right corner versus top left corner, or bottom right and left corners are important when locating clues. All little features within the room must be taken into consideration when trying to locate control sites. As the area gets larger, smaller details become less important. For example when you move from a room to a building the details in the room are not important other than the fact that they may have a closet in them. What becomes more important is the room itself in relationship to other rooms and fixtures in the building. Once you progress to an area outside a building which includes surrounding fields and other building structures, the interior of any area is no longer significant, but outside structures and alleys, roads, and other details relevant to the outside surroundings become important. When the area gets even larger specific details surrounding a particular building or site might become less significant. Things that take on more significance would be roads, trails, streams, bridges, and cliffs, etc., which may become important as handrails for finding where you are going. The greater the distance covered the more general the entire picture becomes and the smaller the area the more specific every detail becomes.

ANTICIPATED OUTCOME

- Sketch maps of simple inside and outside areas
- Have a basic understanding of orienteering symbols
- Interpret map features
- Thumb an orienteering map
- Make good route choice decisions

ACTIVITY ONE

How well can you remember objects that you have seen? Try this simple exercise. Have everyone close their eyes and ask them specific questions about the room they are in. How many details can they remember?

PRE-LESSON DISCUSSION

The following topics should be discussed with the group before beginning the Orienteering Unit.

Brainstorm

What is orienteering?

- Orienteering is navigating one's way through known or unknown terrain with the use of a special map and sometimes a compass.
- Orienteering is both a recreational and an elite sport.
- Orienteering experiences may include any map reading experience such as consulting a street map, a mall directory, or a map of bus routes.
- Orienteering may be experienced in different ways (ski's, running, walking).

Discussion

What is a map? Discuss the different types of maps and what their purposes are.

- A map is a reduced picture of the ground from a bird's eye view. It is a 2 dimensional (or flat) graphic representation of the 3 dimensional world.
- Maps have been created to help people visualize areas before they see them.
- Many types of maps exist; road, topographic (relief), world, directory, transportation, hiking, architecture, tourist, town, and city.
- Maps usually have a title, a scale (for distance calculations), a North directional arrow, a legend (explaining the symbols and colors used on the map) and topic specific detail (hiking trails, vegetation, city plans, etc.).
- Some maps use international symbols and standards so that they can be used throughout the world and by people of many different languages.
- An orienteering map differs from other maps in the following way:

  1. More detail including features such as boulders, small depressions, trails, and vegetation boundaries.
  2. A large scale of a smaller area than most topographic maps.
  3. A magnetic north orientation rather than a true north orientation (eliminating the need to account for magnetic declination)
  4. All symbols and colors are of International Orienteering Federation specifications.

Discuss the various types of orienteering

Because orienteering requires mainly map reading, the type of physical activity may vary: running, walking, canoeing, cycling, skiing, or snowshoeing. Other variations include 24-hour events, and the ever-popular Scandinavian event- night orienteering with headlamps.

Orienting a map by inspection:

Keeping the map oriented is a critical skill in orienteering. The map is oriented when the map features are matched up directionally with the terrain and with the surrounding features.

START   FINISH   START/FINISH

The start location symbol is represented by a triangle, a double circle represents the finish location symbol, and a common start/finish is represented by a triangle inside a circle.

Holding, Folding, and "Thumbing"

Once the map is oriented, fold the map with one fold so that the area where the orienteer is and where the orienteer is going is exposed. Hold the map (usually held in the left hand), in the crux of the index finger and thumb with the thumb on the top surface of the map and the other fingers underneath to give it a "table-like" stability. The orienteer's thumb should be placed on the starting location and then should "follow" along on the main features on the map as the are passed in the terrain.

Map Symbols:

Graphic representations on a map of features in the terrain. For example a large solid black dot is the symbol for a boulder. (See Materials Supplement).

LESSON ONE

THEME
POINT-TO-POINT ORIENTEERING

OBJECTIVE: To practice locating their position on a map. To find control points using a large-scale map.

MATERIALS

- Indoor area with distinct features (doors, tables, chairs, etc.)
- Large scale map of room
- Set of control cards and pencils

PREPARATION

1. Create simple features in the room
2. Plan 12—15 control sites.
3. Mark all the control sites on all the maps with red circles
4. Mark the start/finish with a triangle
5. Create control codes. Each control code identifies a different control. Control codes can be anything you want them to be. For example, selected letters can be unscrambled to create a phrase "Cunning Running"
6. Create the number of controls needed for the activity.

ACTIVITY

1. Evaluate the group's understanding of the map and the symbols used. Look at the large map and ask individual children to identify specific features in the room.
2. Show the group a sample control and how it is going to be symbolized on the map. Discuss that the map is not 3 dimensional and indicate the height range and where the control may be located.
3. Set the map so it is oriented to the room on the floor so everyone can see it.
4. On the map, find the control with number "1" beside it. This is the first control. Walk around the set map until you are looking in the direction of the control as viewed from the start. Pick up the map. The map is set.
5. Go to control 1 and mark down the letter found on the control card. Continue to control 2,3, etc. until all the controls have been visited.

POINT TO POINT ORIENTEERING

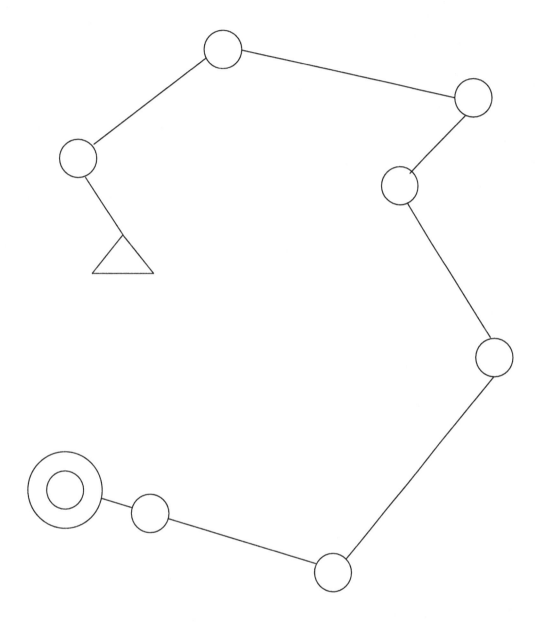

Start at the triangle and follow the lines from one control point to the next until your reach the finish, which is indicated by the double circle.

Nancy Kelly

CONTROL CARD		CONTROL CARD	
1		1	
2		2	
3		3	
4		4	
5		5	
6		6	
7		7	
8		8	
9		9	
10		10	
11		11	
12		12	
13		13	
14		14	
15		15	

LESSON ONE A

THEME
STAR ORIENTEERING

OBJECTIVE: To introduce the concept of a map and basic map reading skills.

MATERIALS

- Indoor area with distinct features
- Large scale map
- Set of control cards and pencils

PREPARATION

1. Create simple symbols for the features in the room.
2. Draw a map of the room on a large piece of paper or cardboard. Begin with the key features such as walls, doors, windows, chairs, tables, mats, etc.
3. Create control sites. In this case letters to spell out "The Thinking Sport". When using a phrase the control card will have the appropriate number of spaces to record each code.
4. Create the number of controls necessary for the activity. In this case 16 letters and thus 16 controls. Number the control in one corner of the control card and put the control code in the other corner.

ACTIVITY

1. Explain the features of the map to the group and place it in the center of the room on the ground oriented to the room.
2. Hand out the control cards and have them put their names on their cards.
3. Explain to them that they should:

   - Read the map carefully
   - Find all the controls in any order
   - Record the control code in the appropriate numbered box by matching the number of the control to the numbered box on their control card
   - Work individually and try not to give away the location of a control
   - Unscramble the coded phrase

4. Encourage everyone to return to the center map frequently to check locations
5. Continue until the majority of the group have completed the course and have unscrambled the coded phrase.
6. For more advanced groups try this variation. Place additional false letters scattered around the room forcing the students to focus more on clear map reading skills.

Time permitting let everyone try to draw a map of the room.

DISCUSSION

Get the group together and go over the activity.

- How did they manage to find out where they were on the map- map/self orientation?
- What was their process of finding the control?
- Which controls were easiest/hardest to find and why?
- Which room features help to read the map?
- What decisions had to be made to find the correct controls?
- Was it difficult trying to draw a 2-dimensional map from the 3-dimensional room?

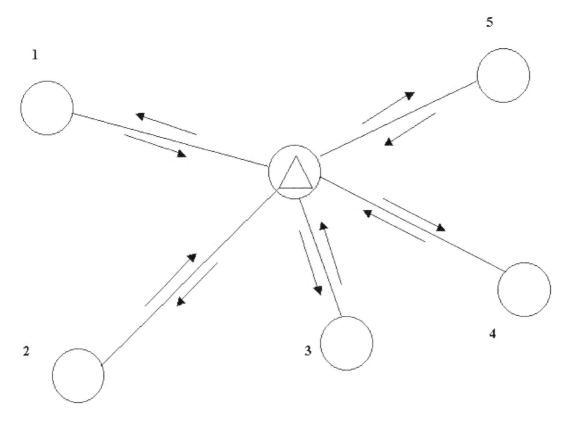

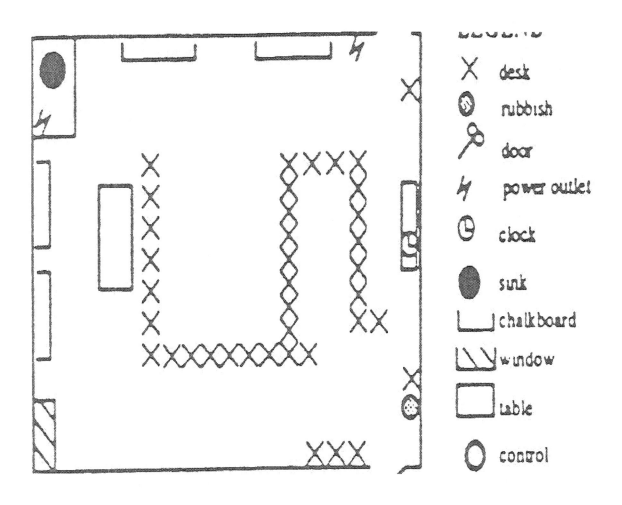

CONTROL CARD		CONTROL CARD	
1		1	
2		2	
3		3	
4		4	
5		5	
6		6	
7		7	
8		8	
9		9	
10		10	
11		11	
12		12	
13		13	
14		14	
15		15	

LESSON TWO

THEME
MOTALA ORIENTEERING

OBJECTIVE: To practice locating control points as a group.

MATERIALS

- Master map of indoor area
- Set of small maps
- Set of control cards and pencils

PREPARARION

1. Plan a variety of control locations; easy and difficult and long and short distances from the start location. Mark them on the master map in a random or non-sequential manner.
2. Have the students mark all the control sites on their maps with a colored pencil.
3. Mark the start/finish with a triangle.
4. Create 3 or more different courses.
5. Create control codes. In this case the control codes are puzzle pieces.
6. Create the number of control sites needed for the activity.

ACTIVITY

Motala orienteering involves using 3 or more different courses and they can be done in any order.

1. Divide the group into 2 teams. Give each team a master map with 12 control sites that they must transcribe onto their own maps.
2. Have the team decide how best to split up the group. This involves team cooperation and planning to figure out who are the quickest as well as the best at navigating.
3. The teams are competing for time to see which team can complete the puzzle first. The teams can use whatever strategy they like to achieve their goal. Everyone in the group must be involved.
4. Try to divide the control sites evenly amongst the members in the team so that each group is trying to locate 3 or 4 control points (puzzle pieces).

5. When each team and group has his or her respective maps, give the signal to start the competition.
6. Go to only the control points on your map and pick up the puzzle piece at the control site.
7. The first team to complete the puzzle wins.

MOTALA ORIENTEERING

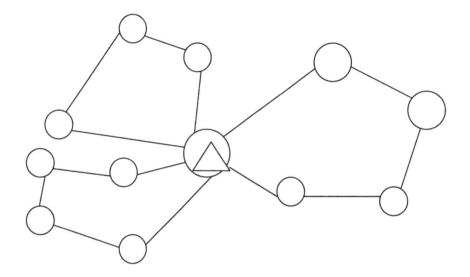

Three different courses with three or four control points for each course. All have the same start and stop point.

LESSON THREE

THEME
MYSTERY ORIENTEERING

OBJECTIVE: Reinforce individual map skills while competing in a "Who done it" game.

MATERIALS

- Master maps of area with different starting points
- Set of small maps
- Set of control cards and pencils

PREPARATION

1. Plan a variety of control locations, easy and difficult throughout the building using building features (doorways, halls, fire escapes, etc.) Mark them on the master map in a random or non-sequential manner.
2. Have the students mark all the control sites on their maps with a colored pencil.
3. Have the class work in a group of 2 or 3 or individually.
4. Mark the start with a triangle. There are 8 to 10 master maps with different starting points.
5. Create control codes. In this case the control codes are clues to a mystery.
6. Create the number of control sites needed for the activity.

ACTIVITY

The scene is set. Someone has found a dead body, but nobody knows where it happened, by whom, or how they were killed (like the game of "CLUE").

1. Give everyone a game card (control card) with the list of possible suspects, weapons that may have been used, and a list of rooms or areas where the crime occurred. The task is to locate the clues and solve the mystery. The clues are scattered around the building.
2. Everyone is given one of the 8 master maps. They are to transcribe all the control points from the master and the starting point onto their individual map.

3. The first task is to locate the starting point, which will tell them what color game card they are to use. By having different starting points this will encourage random searching and discourage teams following each other.
4. All the control points must be located in order to find the solution.
5. Everyone must be able to read a map and navigate his or her way through the building.
6. The control sites can be visited in random order. All of the control sites give clues to solve the mystery.
7. There is a random start but the finish is dependant upon finding all the clues.
8. The first person or team to find all the clues and solve the mystery wins.

DISCUSSION

Were the clues easy or hard to find?

Did you find yourself following other teams or did you stay independent of everyone?

Did you try to guess the answer before you found all of the clues?

Did you have fun?

Would you have used a different way to start the exercise or did this way of starting work?

Did you need help finding some of the clues?

Do you think you could now read an outdoor map and continue to practice orienting the map and thumbing the map?

MYSTERY "O"

Name: _____   Class Period: _____

SUSPECTS	found	found
Mr. Parker		
Ms. Tisdale		
Mrs. Snow		
Dr. Pipps		
Mr. Brown		
WEAPONS		
Knife		
Revolver		
Tire Wrench		
Rope		
Dumb Bell		
ROOMS		
Library		
Auditorium		
Garage		
Hall		
Lounge		
Study		
Kitchen		
Dining Room		
Court Yard		
Elevator		
Laboratory		

Color Codes

Green	Red	Orange	Purple
Yellow	Blue	Black	Brown

Map Numbers

1	2	3	4
5	6	7	8

2003 Orienteering Made Simple

SECTION TWO

ELEMENTARY ORIENTEERING
OUTDOOR MAP SKILLS

Nancy Kelly

SECTION TWO

In order to progress to the next level of orienteering it will be necessary to build on the knowledge and skills from Section One and begin to use larger, more detailed outdoor maps. At this point you will need to be able to:

- Sketch maps of simple outside areas and use symbols to represent features
- Interpret map features including contours
- Identify the line features, handrails, attack points, and collecting features
- Thumb their position on an oriented map
- Understand how to make route choice decisions

ORIENTEERING SYMBOLS

In order to be successful in orienteering it is important to be able to read a map and recognize the different symbols that are used in orienteering. There are a few different activities that you can do with the class to help them learn the symbols and to have fun in the process.

ACTIVITY ONE

Have everyone practice the symbols by using flash cards. Go over the flash cards two times as a group and then try to have the student's name the symbols as you go through the cards a third time. Some groups may be able to do it on the second try.

Play a game of ROUND UP. Place all of the symbols on the ground. Divide the class into two teams. Have the teams stand behind a designated line as you scatter all the symbols on the ground. There should be two complete sets of symbols, one for each team. The first person in each team is given a name of a symbol to find. Their task is to go and retrieve the symbol and bring that card back and give it to the next person on their team who must retrieve the symbol that is written on the back of the first card. This sequence will be followed until all the cards are collected. This can only be done if the cards are picked up in the correct sequence so that the last card that is picked up is blank on the reverse side and all the symbols have been collected.

To prepare for this activity you will need to have two decks of cards with all of the symbols on them and on the back of each symbol will be the name of another symbol not of the symbol on the reverse side. The name of the symbol on the reverse side of every card will indicate the next symbol to find in the game sequence. There is only one solution to this game and if the blank card is picked before all the cards are pick up it will be necessary to back track to try to correct the problem. Try to encourage teamwork to solve the problem and win the game.

ACTIVITY TWO

This involves a handout where symbols are drawn in a story and the fun is in trying to decipher the story by putting the name of the symbol into the story where indicated. An example is A WALK IN THE WOODS.

ACTIVITY THREE

Give everyone in the class a piece of graph paper, which they will use to draw their own map. This map drawing activity will reinforce the understanding of map symbols, cardinal directions, and distance. Students are given the outline of an island in an ocean, N, S, E, and W references are shown on the edges of the map. They will receive directions telling them where to draw in certain symbols on the map. The name of this activity is called MAPPING FANTASY ISLAND. The more advanced the class the more map symbols can be used.

MATERIALS SUPPLEMENT

VEGETATION BOUNDARY	PERMANENT BENCH
PERMANTENT TABLE	UNCROSSABLE MARSH
POND	CLIFF FACE
CONIFEROUS TREES	DECIDUOUS TREES
TREE STUMP	DRY DITCH
TRAIL/STREAM CROSSING	FENCE CORNER

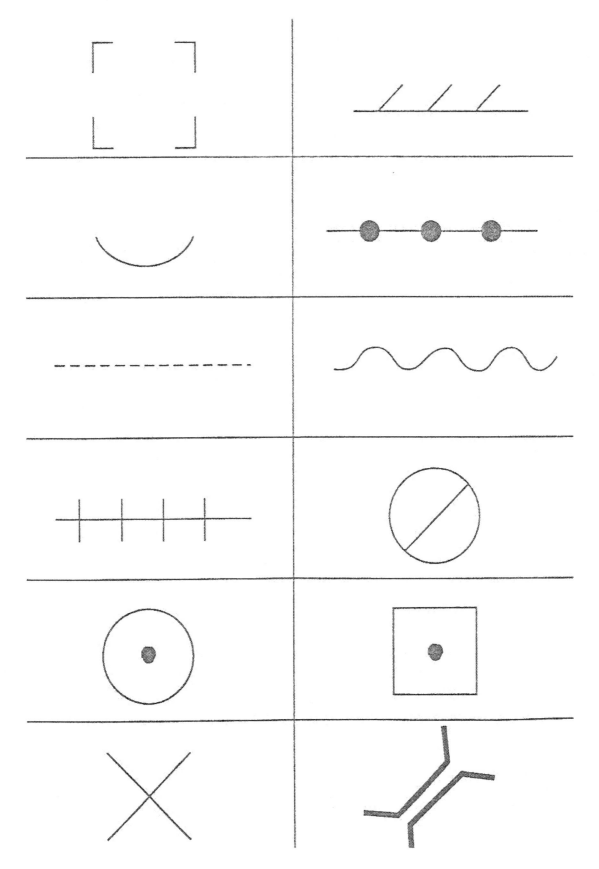

RUIN	FENCE
DEPRESSION	WALL
TRAIL	STREAM
POWERLINE	SEWER
SIGN POST	FLAG POLE
ROOTSTOCK	BRIDGE

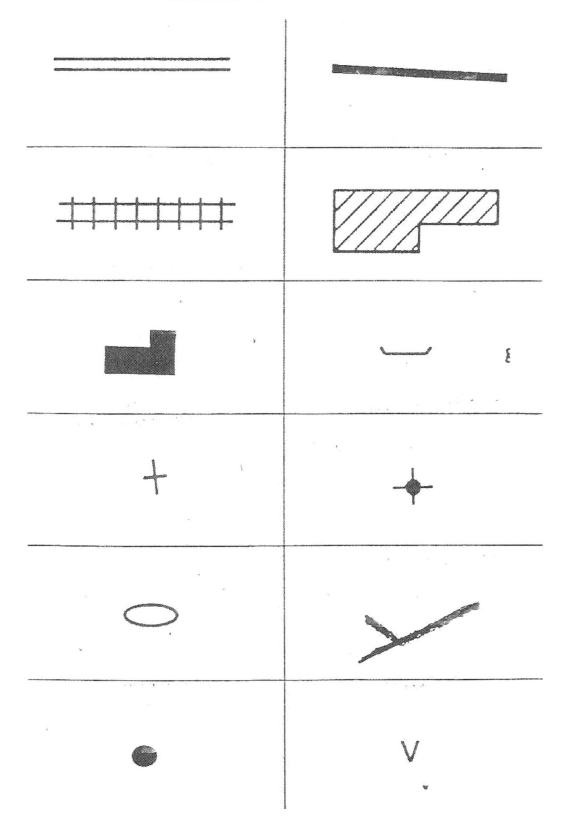

MAIN ROAD	DIRT ROAD
RAILWAY	PARKING LOT
BUILDING	GOAL POST
PLAYGROUND EQUIPMENT	LIGHTPOLE
SMALL HILL (KNOLL)	TRAIL JUNCTION
BOULDER	PIT

A WALK IN THE WOODS

Once upon a time there were three students who decided to go for a walk in the woods.

They left their ◼ and had to cross the ⋯⋅⋅⋅ . They passed many 🌲

and 🌳 as they walked along the ▬▬▬ . They followed a ⌒⌒⌒

which eventually brought them to a ∠ . They traveled on the ‒ ‒ ‒ ‒ which came

to a ▬ . The only way they could get across was by going over a ⋈ . Once they

got to the other side of the ⬤ , they came to a ‒⋅‒⋅‒ . They went through and

came upon a ⌐ ¬ . Inside the ⌐ ¬ there were ⌐⌐ and ⊤

, but they were not in good condition. There were also many large ● which must

have come from the ⌐⊓⊓⌐ that was on the North side of the ⌐ ¬ . They

decided to keep going because it was starting to get dark and there were no ✦

.

They had to climb a ⬭ but at the bottom they came to an 〰 so they

had to try to go around it. They were beginning to think they would never get out of the

woods when they came upon a ▭ . They saw a ⊙ and they

realized they were almost home.

ACTIVITY THREE

MAPPING FANTASY ISLAND

- Start out drawing a large island on a piece of graph and mark N., S., E., & W. Each box of the graph paper will measure one mile.
- A trail starts at the NW corner of the island and goes S 5 miles and then runs E along the top of a cliff for 3 miles until it reaches a pond.
- The trail then goes directly N until it reaches a bridge at the waters edge that is used to bring cars out to the ferry.
- To the E of the bridge is a large cliff with a pit at the SW corner of the cliff. A stream runs from the opening (point) of the pit to the pond.
- A trail goes across the stream 1 mile S of the pit.
- The trail starts from the trail that was traveling N and continues E for 10 miles from the stream until it meets a ruin. The ruin has 4 large boulders around it.
- From the southern most part of the ruin a stonewall goes S until it meets a dirt road 7 miles S of the ruin. The dirt road starts 8 miles west of the wall and continues E to the shore where there is a light pole.
- A main road starts from the light pole and travels SW for 13 miles.
- The road crosses over a large stream (bridge) at 9 miles and then continues until it reaches a signpost.
- The road then travels NW for 13 miles until it meets the dirt road.
- Just S of the V in the road is a marsh.
- The stonewall that opened at the dirt road travels S for 5 miles until it comes to a fence junction.
- At the fence junction there are several fallen trees (rootstock).
- The fence travels NE for 5 miles until it comes to a large coniferous tree along the N side of the dirt road.
- The fence also travels NW 5 miles until it comes to a large oak tree on the N side of the dirt road.
- The dirt road stops at a building with a parking lot on the west side of the building.
- A flagpole is just north of the building.
- On the NW side of the parking lot is a large field with soccer goals at each end.
- S of the soccer field is a playground.
- A vegetation boundary runs along the W and S sides of the playground.
- To the S of the building there are 2 power lines.
- To the W of the soccer field there are 2 table and 4 benches.
- There is also a sewer system at the SW corner of the vegetation boundary.

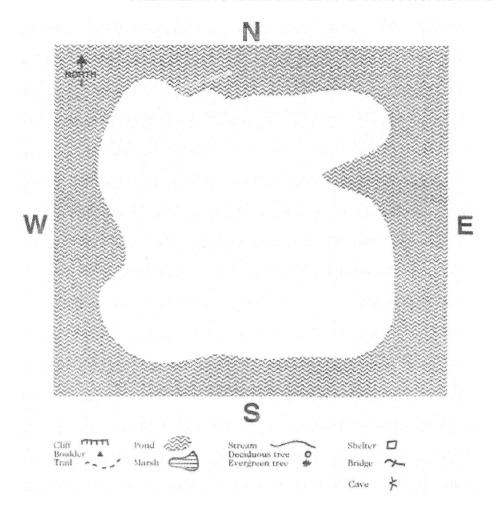

Go through the instructions several times so that the students understand the process. A variation of this activity can be used More or fewer map symbols can be used, especially simple terrain features (depression, pit, knoll, hill, gully). Also, color can be used to show features as well: BLACK for man-made features and rock features; BROWN for contour features like hills, knolls, depressions, etc.; BLUE for water, marsh, stream, lake, etc.; GREEN for thick forest; YELLOW for open areas like a field or meadow.

LESSON FOUR

THEME
TRIVIA ORIENTEERING

OBJECTIVE: To encourage outdoor map reading skills.

MATERIALS

- Maps of an outside area
- Set of blank control cards to answer the trivia questions at each control site
- Set of pencils

PREPARATION

1. Photocopy maps of an outdoor area containing a legend.
2. Make a master map containing all of the control points circled.
3. Hand out copies of the master trivia answer sheet.
4. Review symbols, handrails, attack points, and collecting features.

ACTIVITY

Trivia orienteering is a form of orienteering in which the proof of visitation to a control is provided by answering a trivia question about the location.

1. Explain to the group that they are looking for trivia questions that correspond to a control location.
2. Give everyone an outdoor map and have him or her transcribe all of the control sites onto their maps.
3. The control sites can be visited in any order. If you find the control site but cannot answer the question, write the question in the appropriate box.
4. Each control site will have a number and a question next to it. Make sure you put the correct answer next to the proper number on the control card.

TRIVIA ORIENTEERING SAMPLE SHEET

Trivia Orienteering Question Sheet

#	Control Trivial Question	Answer
1.	Name a state that starts and ends in the same letter.	
2.	Another name for 12 dozen is what?	
3.	How many months have only 30 days?	

Master Trivia Orienteering Answer Sheet

#	Control Trivia Question	Answer
1.	Name a state that starts and ends in the same letter.	**Ohio**
2.	Another name for 12 dozen is what?	**Gross**
3.	How many months have only 30 days?	**4**

Trivia Orienteering Question Sheet

#	Trivia Question	Answer
1.		
2.		
3.		
4.		
5.		
6.		
7.		
8.		
9.		
10.		
11.		
12.		

LESSON FIVE

THEME
PROJECT ORIENTEERING

OBJECTIVE: To challenge map reading abilities and to encourage sportsmanlike behavior in a competitive, timed activity.

MATERIALS

- Master map with clearly defined boundaries
- Set of sample maps to be transcribed onto
- 10-15 controls with a description of the project at every station
- Stop watch

PREPARATION

1. Plan a variety of control locations; easy and difficult; and short and long distances form the start location. Mark them on the master maps in a random or non-sequential manner for the students to copy from.
2. Assign a task or project at each control.
3. Secure control descriptions and control cards at each of the locations.
4. Place all the equipment necessary to complete the task at each of the controls.

ACTIVITY

1. Hand out blank maps and have the students copy the control locations onto their own map.
2. Explain that there is a stunt or task to do at each of the control sites and proof of arrival at a control site will depend upon their group completing the task.
3. Explain that each member of the group should plan a strategy for locating the control point in the least amount of time and making sure that they can complete the task.
4. The controls may be found in any order.
5. Stress group navigation.
6. Explain that there will be bonus points added to their team's score by not exceeding the time limit as well as for completing the task at each of the controls they find.

7. Recommend that everyone studies the map and plans a strategy before taking off from the start.
8. Encourage participants to finish within the specified time. The whistle will indicate when time is up.
9. This activity can be done as a mass start or random start as long as each team receives a start time and the time lapse is calculated accordingly.

Sample course could include these projects:

1. Count how many steps you use to go 100 meters on the track (set up two markers to have them pace out).
2. Try to throw a tennis ball into a basket sitting on top of a basketball hoop.
3. Climb the bleachers and place a team marker on the top railing.
4. Assemble a simple puzzle.
5. Make a pyramid of blocks.
6. Hit a foam golf ball into a hoop.
7. Answer a riddle.
8. Collect a leaf and bring it with you.

Encourage team- work and good sportsmanship. Discourage cheating.

DISCUSSION

- Which controls were easy or difficult to locate?
- Did you use handrails, collecting features, and attack points for any of the controls?
- What were the effects of physical participation at the control sites?
- Which controls were the most popular/unpopular?
- Could you read your map while moving?
- Did you "thumb" your way along?
- Did the other groups distract you?

LESSON SIX

THEME
SCORE ORIENTEERING

OBJECTIVE: To encourage route choice strategies with a time constraint.

MATERIALS

- Set of blank maps with clearly defined boundaries, such as roads, fences, or buildings
- Master maps
- 15-20 controls with codes and numbers
- Set of control cards
- Set of control descriptions and control point values
- Stop watch and whistle

PREPARATION

1. Plan a variety of control locations: easy and difficult; and short and long distances from the start location. Mark them on the map in a random or non-sequential manner.
2. Assign a point value for each control based on its level of difficulty and distance from the start.
3. Secure control cards to maps.
4. Assign a time limit, selecting a time that will allow most controls to be found, but not all of them.
5. Randomly number the controls on the map.
6. Set control.

ACTIVITY

This is one of the most versatile forms of Orienteering because it lends itself to any time frame, any size area, and will accommodate mass starting. It is also easy to organize. This exercise highlights the need to carefully select routes, which will cover as much terrain as possible within a specific time limit. The object is to collect as many points as possible within the time limit. Points are deducted for going overtime; for example, 5 points are deducted for every minute or part of a minute late

1. Hand out maps and control cards. Copy the control locations from the master maps onto the blank maps.
2. Explain that this is a timed event and points are awarded for finding as many controls as possible within a time limit.
3. Recommend that everyone study the map and use strategy before taking off in order to find the most controls and the greatest number of points within the time period.
4. The controls may be found in any order.
5. Have the participants record the control code on their control card.
6. Explain that a whistle will blow when 4 minutes are left and that 2 long blows will indicate that time is up. Make sure that everyone understands the timing system and the importance of returning to the starting point before time elapses.
7. The start can be mass or random, but make sure everyone receives a start time and a finishing time and calculate accordingly.

POST ACTIVITY DISCUSSION

- Trade control cards with another team and calculate someone else's total points
- What strategies were used? What worked?
- What handrails, collecting features or other information were most helpful?
- What were the effects of physical and time limitations?

SCORE ORIENTEERING
SAMPLE SHEET

TIME LIMIT:			15 minutes
PENALTY:			**5 points perminute late**
Control #	**Control Letter**	**Value**	**Control Description**
1.		**5**	**Opening in Fence**
2.		**15**	**Gate Post**
3.		**10**	**Flag Pole Base**
13.		**20**	**Lamp Post**
14.		**5**	**Street Name Post**
15.		**10**	**Stop Sign**
	Less		**=**
Total Points		**Penalty Points**	**Final Score**

Score Orienteering

Time Limit:15 minutes

Penalty: 5 pts. Per minute late

Control #	Control Letter	Control Value	Control Discription
1			
2			
3			
4			
5			
6			
7			
8			
9			
10			
11			
12			
13			
14			
15			
16			
17			
18			
19			
20			
	Total Points		
	Penalty Pts.	-	
	Final Score	=	

2003 Orientering Made Simple

40

THEME
TEAM RELAY ORIENTEERING

OBJECTIVE: To challenge map-reading abilities and encourage sportsmanship like behavior on a competitive, timed activity.

MATERIALS

- One map per team of 3-4
- Set of control cards
- One master control card
- 12 controls with codes and numbers
- Team Recorder Sheet

PREPARATION

1. Prepare 4 short courses (or more depending upon the number of teams) of 3-4 controls in a clover -leaf pattern with a common start/finish area.
2. Each course should only take 3-4 minutes to provide more active participation by everyone.
3. Have a master card with the proper controls for each course to cross check accuracy upon completion.
4. Teams should prepare their own maps from the master maps.
5. Set controls.

ACTIVITY

1. Have everyone on the team place their names on the control card.
2. Begin at the start/finish area and all team switches are to be made in this area.
3. Have each member carry the map with them to the control site and have them "follow" their way to the control on the map.
4. Make sure to mark the proper control code in the proper box on the control card.

Alternate variation allows the participants to set up the course.

Make this a three day event. The first day the students will form into three teams. Each team will be assigned an area of the fields around the school that they will set up their orienteering course on. They are to have 8 control sites (you may need to set up more or less depending upon the number of people on a team) that should be clearly defined on their maps. Make sure that they only mark clear boundaries (corner of fence, edge of building, goal posts, bleachers, sign posts, etc).

Day Two the teams will go out and put the control markers at the control sites. Use the rip-away florescent caution tape that you can find at any hardware store (they come in different colors) to secure the cards at each location. It is a good idea to number each of the strips that are put out so they know that they picked up the right control marker. Give each team about 10-15 minutes to complete this task.

After this is done have the teams exchange maps with one of the other teams. On the signal (whistle) one team member from each team will go out to try to locate one of the controls. When they do they should run back give the map to another person on their team who will then try to locate another control site. Continue in this fashion until everyone on the team has gone out to get a control card or all 8 controls have been found. Record the time it takes each team to retrieve all 8 control markers.

Day Three will be just like day two but each team will take another team's map and try to locate the controls from that section of the field. Record the times it takes each team to retrieve all 8 control markers.

Calculate the two-day total to determine which team accomplished the task in the least amount of time.

The transition site should be at one location and the person on the team who is retrieving the control card should carry the map with them to the control site. Each class will have their own set of maps and control cards which should be collected at the end of the period.

THEME
CROSS-COUNTRY ORIENTEERING

OBJECTIVE: To challenge map reading abilities in an activity suited for a large area that is partially wooded.

MATERIALS

- Master map with clearly defined boundaries
- Set of blank maps and control cards and control descriptions.
- 8-12 controls hidden within the wooded area.

PREPARATION

1 The course should range in length from 1-2.5km with 8-12 controls. The distance to the first control should be a little longer than the rest in order to spread participants out at the beginning.
2 Avoid placing controls, which force participants to double-back.
3 The controls must be placed sequentially and they must be found in the order indicated on the map.

ACTIVITY

This is the "traditional" Orienteering used for most competitions.

1. All control must be found in the order indicated on the map.
2. Have everyone place their name on their control card and attach a map with the control points and control descriptions to it.
3. Begin at the start triangle indicated on their map.
4. Each member should carry the maps with them and "follow" or "thumb" their way from one control to the next.
5. Make sure to match the control site with their control description before marking the control code on their control card. Make sure the proper numbered box is marked on the control card.
6. When the course is completed hand in the control card so that it can be scored for accuracy.
7. This activity can be done in pairs or individually and may be started with a staggered start of 30-second intervals, or as a mass start.

Cross-country Orienteering is the standard competitive form of orienteering and requires a little more organization and more time than the previous two. Try to discourage teams from following one another or putting controls in repeating or backtracking patterns. This will prevent participants going to control 4 seeing people leaving 4 to go to 5. In other words, control 4 requires little or no orienteering skill to locate. The way to prevent this from happening is by adding a control. Remember the fun is in the discovery.

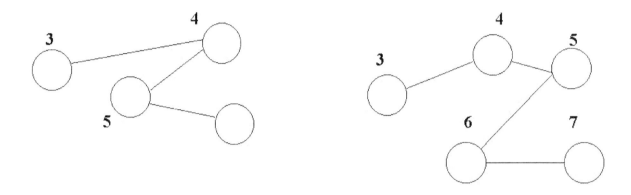

CONTROL CARD

CONTROL CARD

SECTION THREE

INTERMEDIATE ORIENTEERING USING A COMPASS

READING A MAP

The ability to map read and to relate the map to the actual features on the ground is the basis of all orienteering and must be practiced constantly.

The orienteer must make many decisions as to the best route to follow. This demands the ability to:

- Read fine contours and relate to actual landforms
- Judge actual distance in relation to map scale
- Recognize features on the map
- Mentally tick off features as they are reached
- Constantly relate the map to the ground to ensure accuracy in navigation

The use of the compass in orienteering in conjunction with the map will develop a very high degree of skills.

OBJECTIVES:

- Become familiar with terminology used to read a map such as longitude and latitude, etc.
- Recognize directions on the map and know how to locate places based on their location to other objects or places around it.
- Become familiar with compass bearings and how to set ones bearings to locate places.
- Learn how to estimate distances on a map by using step counting.

DIRECTIONAL AND COMPASS SKILLS

Compass Parts and Functions:

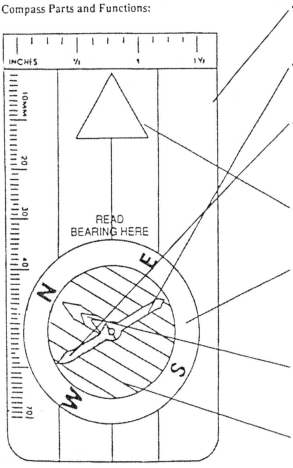

- Base Plate: the transparent surface which forms the base of the protractor baseplate compass. The direction-of-travel arrow and a measurement scale are engraved on it.
- Magnetic Needle: the flat red and white needle on a pivot in the middle of the housing. The red end of the needle will always rest pointing to magnetic north when held motionless in the horizontal plane.
- Magnetic North: the direction which the red end of the magnetic needle points to. The needle is affected by the earth's magnetic field and thus the red end of the magnetic needle will always point to magnetic north rather than true (geographic) north. All orienteering maps are drawn to magnetic north.
- Direction-of-travel Arrow: an engraved straight line which runs from the centre of the housing rim to the front edge of the base plate to indicate the direction of travel once the map and compass have been oriented.
- Housing: the round dial which contains the magnetic needle. The rim of the protractor compass housing rotates manually, identifies north and the other cardinal directions, and is divided into 360 degrees. The orienting arrow and parallel orienting lines are engraved on the base of the housing. The housing is filled with a fluid to help stabilize the magnetic needle.
- Orienting Arrow: engraved on the base of the compass housing and points directly to the housing's north marking. The compass is oriented when the red end of the magnetic needle is aligned with and is pointing in the same direction as the orienting arrow.
- Orienting Lines: engraved in the bottom of the housing and run parallel to the orienting arrow.

GOLD CHALLENGE - WRITTEN COMPONENT

Name: _____

COMPASS KNOWLEDGE

Correctly identify 5 compass parts by connecting the term with the part by drawing a line.

1. compass housing

2. direction-of-travel arrow

3. magnetic N needle

4. orienting arrow

5. magnetic north lines

6. measurement scale

Correctly match 5 compass functions.

7. orienting arrow   _____ red end always points magnetic north

8. compass housing   _____ engraved in the housing and runs parallel to north

9. magnetic needle   _____ points to housing's north marking

10. direction-of-travel arrow   _____ rotates to change bearing direction

11. measurement scale   _____ helps with measuring paces on the map

12. orienting lines   _____ followed once the map and compass are oriented

READING A MAP (1)

Study the map of the United States on Sheet 4 and try to answer correctly the following questions.

1. In what state do you live? _____

2. What is the capital of your state?_____

3. What states border your state?_____

4. Which states touch the Gulf of Mexico?_____

5. What ocean is east of the United States?_____

6. What ocean is west of the United States?_____

7. What country is north of the United States?_____

8. Which states touch the Pacific Ocean?_____

9. What state is south of South Dakota?_____

10. What state is north of New Mexico?_____

11. What country is south of Arizona?_____

12. Circle the names of any of the following states which are west of Illinois: California - Pennsylvania - West Virginia - Kansas - Louisiana - Maine Tennessee

13. Circle the names of any of the following states that do <u>not</u> touch the Great Lakes: New York - Indiana - Iowa - Minnesota - Vermont - New Jersey Michigan

READING A MAP (2)

1. **New York is located in the: NE, SE, SW, NW**

2. **Texas is located in the: N, S, E, W**

3. **Find a four (4) letter state in the west>_____**

4. **What state is the most NW?_____**

5. **What state is the most NE?_____**

6. **What state is the most SE?_____**

7. **What state is the most SW?_____**

8. **What state is 100° longitude and 40° latitude?_____**

9. **What is at 30° latitude and 80° longitude?_____**

10. **What degree latitude and longitude do you live in?_____**

11. **What degree latitude and longitude is Nevada? _____**

12. **How far is it from New York to California?_____**

13. **How far is it from Delaware to Nebraska?_____**

14. **If you travel 600 miles west of Iowa where will you be? _____**

Name _____   Date _____

READING A MAP   (Sheet 4)

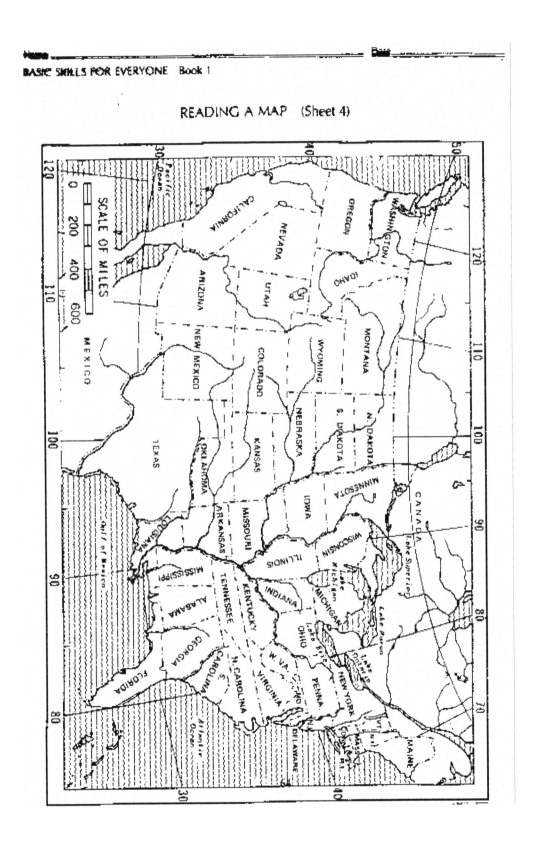

SCALE AND DISTANCE

Maps are, by necessity, drawn to scale and it is this scale, which determines the distance between points on the actual ground.

SCALE

The scale of the map indicates the distance between points shown on the map. At a map scale of 1:1000, points 1 cm apart on the map are10 meters apart on the ground.

- 1:2000 1 cm on the map equals 20 meters on the ground
- 1:2500 1 cm on the map equals 25 meters on the ground
- 1:5000 1 cm on the map equals 50 meters on the ground
- 1:10,000 1 cm on the map equals 100 meters on the ground
- 1:15,000 1 cm on the map equals 150 meters on the ground

ACTIVITIES

These activities will help develop a sense of the relationship between distance on the map and the actual distance on the ground.

- Using any available maps with a clear scale practice measuring the distance on the map and use the scale to calculate the actual distance on the ground.
- The instructor marks out 100 m on a field with a marker at each end. Using double pace counting, i.e., counting each time the right or left foot hits the ground, participants carry out the following exercises:

1. Count the number of double paces while walking the 100 meters and repeat until consistent.
2. Count double paces while running easily, as in a cross-country point-to-point event.
3. Where the terrain is suitable, individuals record their own double pace averages for running over the 100 m in the following types of terrain:

   Open, flat spaces
   Up hill country
   Broken ground areas
   Down hill country

There is still more knowledge that needs to be acquired on how to estimate distance, and this is we will learn by "STEP-COUNTING".

This is a very old technique of judging how far away things are. The Roman soldiers used this technique and counted 'double steps' in groups of 1000. This was called the 'mille passus' in Latin, and this is where the word mile came from and the actual distance.

To practice 'step-counting' we will need to be in an area of at least 100 meters. We will need a 100 meter tape, some markers, paper, and pencil.

Here is the practice

1. Walk the 100 meters and count every time the right foot comes to the ground. Write down the answer.
2. Walk back again, count, and write down the answer.
3. Repeat 1 and 2 again. Add these figures together and divide by 4 to obtain your personal step-count figure for walking 100 meters.
4. Repeat these same procedures, but this time ran at a steady 'marathon' pace. The average figure you obtain this time will be your step-count figure for running 100 meters.
5. Try this same process but do it in rough terrain.

Points to note: Don't over-stride when walking and don't run 100 meters at a dash speed.

Exercise

Use the chart below to calculate your result

Number of DOUBLE STEPS in 100 m

	Open Space	Rough Area
Walking		
Try 1		
Try 2		
Try 3		
Try 4		
Average		
Running		
Try 1		
Try 2		
Try 3		
Try 4		
Average		

All maps are reduced to a scale. In the case of these exercises the answers are based on a map that has a scale of 1:25,000. That means that the map has been reduced 25,000 times. Therefore, for every unit on the exercise map there are 25,000 units on the ground covering the same distance. Because map scales are usually in 1,000's it is convenient to think metric when we want to estimate distance. An easy way to remember how to change different map scales into meters is to take away the last three zeros. The number left tells you the number of meters.

Hence on this exercise:
   1mm = 25 meters on the ground
   10mm = 250 meters on the ground
   40mm = 1,000meters on the ground

Exercise 1

How far on the ground are these distances on a 1:25,000 scale map?

Distance	Answer in meters
a. 1mm	
b. 2mm	
c. 3mm	
d. 5mm	
e. 8mm	
f. 13mm	
g. 28mm	

Exercise 2

How far on the map (scale 1:25,000) are these distances on the ground?

Distance	
a. 50m	
b. 100m	
c. 125m	
d. 300m	
e. 550m	
f. 1,000m	
g. 1,250m	

Exercise 3

Make sure to measure from the beginning of one control to the beginning of another control or from the end of one control to the end of another control. Do not measure from the beginning of one control to the end of another control because this could add 5 mm which is equivalent to 125 meters. This exercise is based on a scale of 1:25,000. Measure the distance in millimeters and convert to meters for each distance.

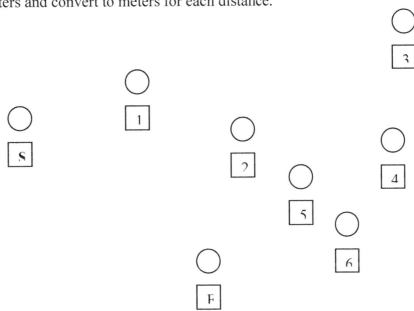

DIRECTION	MILLIMETER	METERS
S to 1		
1 to 2		
2 to 3		
3 to 4		
4 to 5		
5 to 6		
6 to F		

Exercise 4
Carefully find all of the 'CONTROL POINTS' on the PRACTICE MAP. Read the control point definitions to check that you have the correct place.
Answer the questions in the table below by careful measuring.

How far is it between?		Answer in meters

A. Bridge	B. Field Corner	
C. Building	D. Ruin	
E. Power line	F. Marsh	
G. Boulder	H. Cliff	
J. Pond	K. Hill Summit	
L. Waterfall	M. Stream Junction	

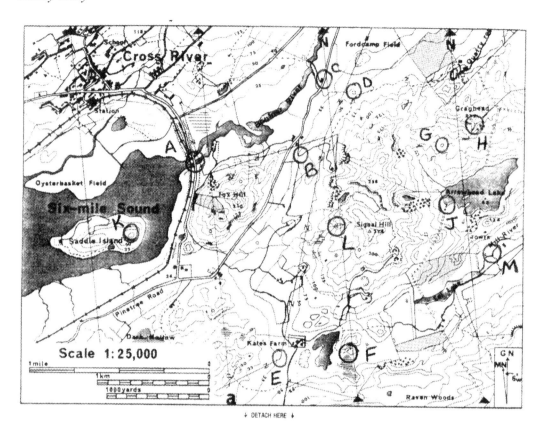

↓ DETACH HERE ↓

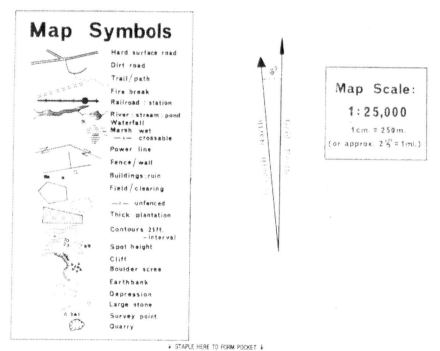

↓ STAPLE HERE TO FORM POCKET ↓

ORIENTING THE COMPASS

1. CARDINAL DIRECTIONS
2. COMPASS PARTS
3. ORIENTEERING BY COMPASS

OBJECTIVE: To introduce directional terms and basic compass and map skills.

Review the four cardinal directions and relate them to the four cardinal points on the compass. Know the inter-cardinal directions as well.

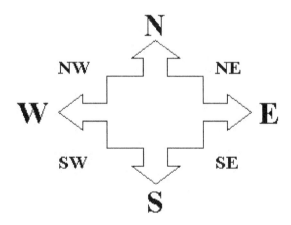

CARRYING A COMPASS:

- Loop compass cord around wrist. Hold the compass in one hand.
- Place the compass level in the palm of your hand with the direction-of travel arrow pointing straight ahead, in line with the center of the body and about waist high.
- Keep the compass level or the needle may get stuck and not move properly.

EXERCISE ONE: FACING THE CARDINAL POINTS

Set the compass to each of the four cardinal points and in each case turn the body and the compass to face them. For example, line up the N on the compass housing with the direction-of-travel arrow. While holding the compass as explained rotate your body until the magnetic needle is aligned with and points in the same direction as the orienting arrow. You will now be facing north.

EXERCISE TWO: DIAL-A-BEARING GAME

Call out a bearing (e.g. 115). Each student must orient their compass to that bearing and face it. Try a number of different bearings with the students.

EXERCISE THREE: LANDMARK BEARINGS

Face a landmark. Aim the compass's direction-of-travel arrow at the landmark and orient the compass.

Compass Direction Exercise

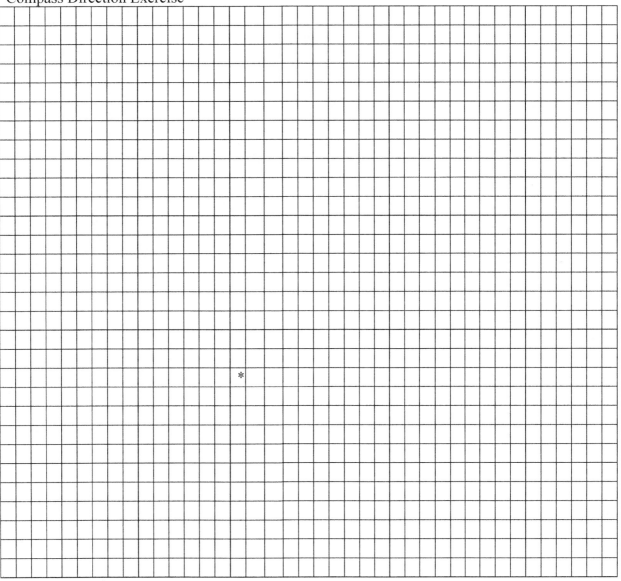

Start at *

1 square = 100 Meters

1. 100 N	8. 200 E	15. 200 W	22. 400 S
2. 200 W	9. 300 N	16. 100 S	23. 400 NW
3. 200 NE	10. 200 NE	17. 200 E	24. 400 SW
4. 200 E	11. 200 SE	18. 200 SE	25. 400 N
5. 100 N	12. 300 S	19. 200 W	26. 200 W
6. 200 W	13. 200 E	20. 100 S	
7. 200NE	14. 200 SE	21. 200 W	

TAKING A COMPASS BEARING FROM A MAP

- In order to read a map more easily, the map should always be oriented to the terrain.
- Orienteering maps have parallel lines, which run south to north over the map. These lines, known a Magnetic North Lines, help to establish the other three cardinal directions and act as a guide to determine north with a compass.
- Rotate the housing until the orienteering arrow points toward the direction-of-travel arrow.
- Place the compass level on the map aligning the base-plate edge with the magnetic north lines and hold the map and compass firmly together. Turn your body until the magnetic needle is aligned with the orienting arrow and points in the same direction as the magnetic north lines on the map. The map is now oriented and the compass may be taken off the map.
- Allow the magnetic needle to settle. Because the needle is fluid it must be given an opportunity to settle before it is read.

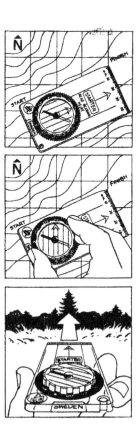

SETTING A MAP

The map is set when the symbols on the map are in direct relationship to the physical features on the ground. When setting a map with a compass, place the compass on the map. The map is then turned until the magnetic north lines are parallel to and pointing in the same direction as the red end of the magnetic needle.

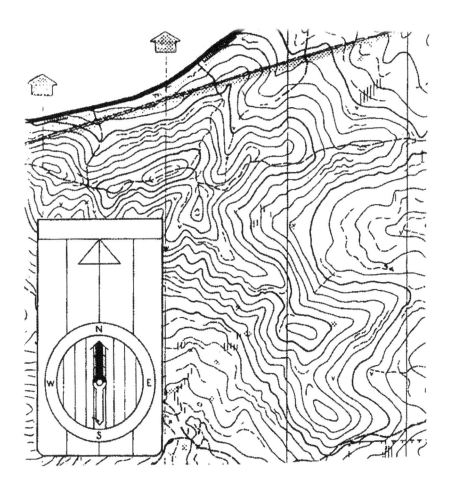

Taking a bearing from a map.

In terrain with few features it is often necessary to use this technique. The following steps are taken:

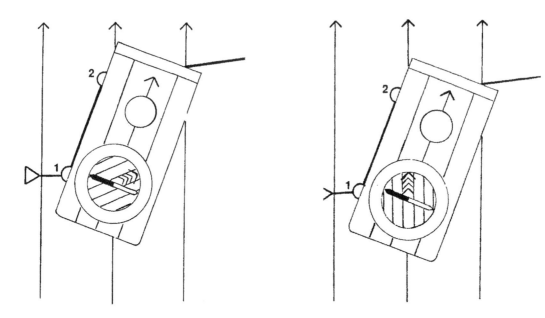

Step 1: Place the compass on the map with the edge joining the two controls. The travel arrow must lie in the desired direction of travel.

Step 2: Turn the compass housing so that the orienting lines run parallel to the meridian lines on the map.

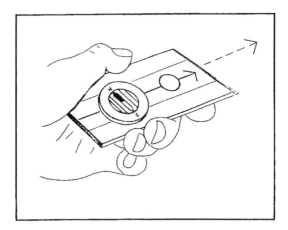

Step 3: Take the compass off the map and hold horizontal and square to the body at waist height, Turn your body until the red magnetic needle sits over the orienting arrow.

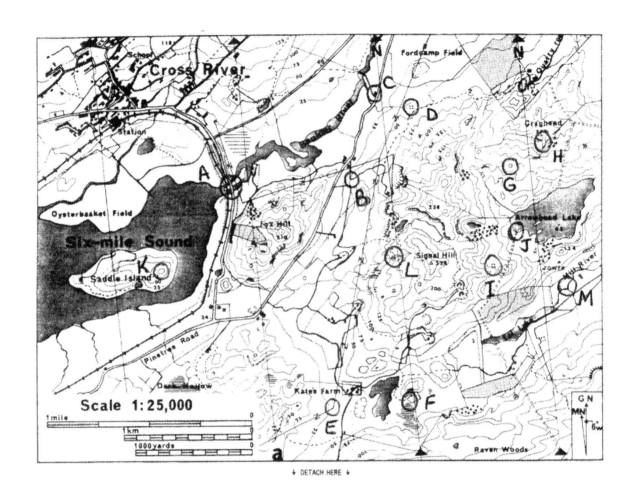

↓ DETACH HERE ↓

Directions			Degrees	Meters
A	→	B		
B	→	C		
C	→	D		
D	→	E		
E	→	F		
F	→	G		
G	→	H		
H	→	I		
I	→	J		
J	→	K		
K	→	L		
L	→	M		
M	→			
	→			
	→			

EXERCISE FOUR:

SCHOOL-YARD COMPASS GAME

The game may be played by small or large groups. The space required is about 100ft. X 100ft. The course consists of eight stakes placed at different compass bearings from a center stake. Each player is told to start at the center and to proceed to 6 different bearings and making the code word.

Another version is to start at E and proceed to the other bearings to make a code word.

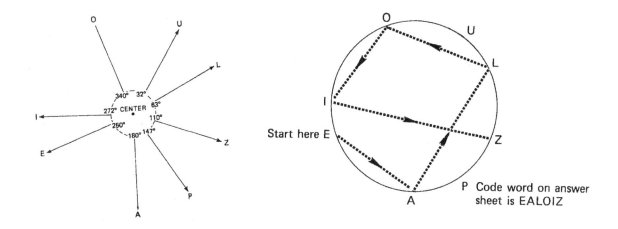

EXERCISE FIVE: CLOVERLEAF ORIENTEERING

From a common start try to navigate by precision compass and pace counting to a control and then navigate to the next control and so on. Each control may be identified by a control description to help them along the way.

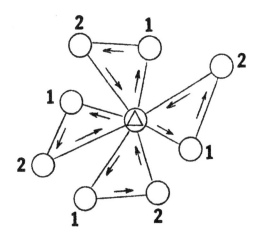

MAP SKILLS

READING CONTOURS

It is important to know whether you will be climbing, descending, or on flat ground as you approach a control. One of the most difficult map reading problems is to visualize the landform patterns that contour lines represent and to relate the pattern of contour lines on the map to the terrain. Key features to look for:

- Contour lines FURTHER APART represent a gentler slope
- Contour lines CLOSER TOGETHER represent a steep slope
- Contour lines MERGING show a very steep slope and /or cliffs
- Contour lines CLOSED around reflect hills or knolls
- Contour lines CLOSED around with slope lines shown represent depressions.

a. Depression
b. Hill/Knoll
c. Flat Ground
d. Spur
e. Re-entrant
f. Steep Slope
g. Gentle Slope

Nancy Kelly

Landforms:

There are many different landforms, each with its own name. These are often used at control sites in orienteering and are identified by control descriptions.

- Re-entrant: A small gull or valley with no permanent watercourse
- Depression: A hollow with higher ground on all sides
- Knoll: A small hill
- Saddle: A low lying dip between two higher points
- Spur: A small ridge, usually steep and lying off a main ridge

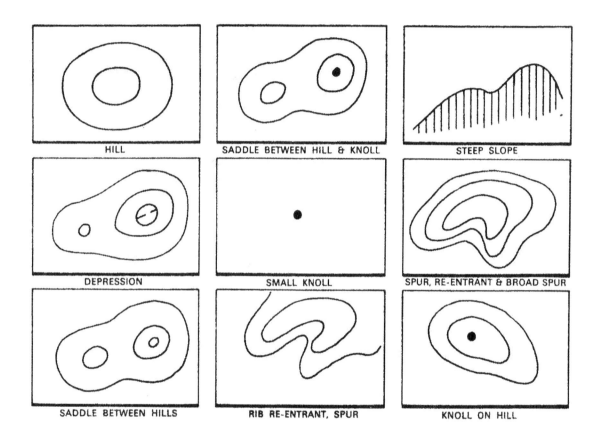

HILL	SADDLE BETWEEN HILL & KNOLL	STEEP SLOPE
DEPRESSION	SMALL KNOLL	SPUR, RE-ENTRANT & BROAD SPUR
SADDLE BETWEEN HILLS	RIB RE-ENTRANT, SPUR	KNOLL ON HILL

PUTTING IT ALL TOGETHER

Orienteering is all about choosing the best route and then using appropriate navigation techniques to travel between controls. While the shortest distance between controls is a straight line it is often not the easiest or fastest route. By following the route of least resistance the distance traveled may be greater but faster in terms of time.

ACTIVITIES

Path of least resistance

Evaluate each of the routes shown on the following map taking into account run ability and ease of navigation.

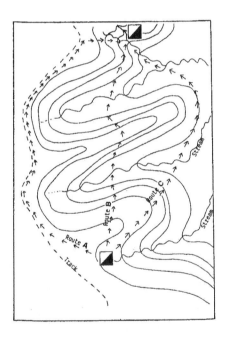

Contouring

Hill climbing is very tiring and a route involving ups and downs will sap energy. It is better to work out alternative routes using contouring techniques to maintain height.

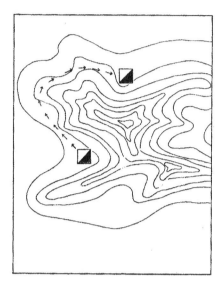

Using handrails

Many different forms of handrails can be identified. The obvious ones are roads, tracks, fences, streams and firebreaks but other features such as ridges, vegetation boundaries and valleys can be extremely helpful. On an orienteering map identify as many handrails as possible.

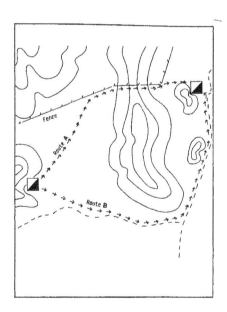

Aiming Off

In situations where the line of travel will meet collecting feature, it is advisable to aim off to ensure you know which way to turn when you reach the collecting feature.

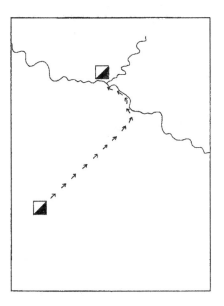

Attack Points

An attack point is a well-defined feature such as a track junction, streambed, pond or hill. To be effective, the attack point should be reasonably close to the control. Once the attack point has been found, very carefully navigate to locate the control.

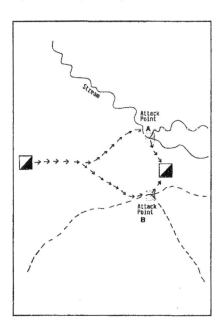

Traffic Lights

Travel from one control to the next can be likened to traffic lights.

- Green: Once a route choice has been made progress is fast to the nearest handrail or collecting feature
- Orange: As the end of a handrail is approached and an attack point has been selected extra care must be taken
- Red: Travel from the attack point to the control must be done very carefully using a compass bearing or fine navigation.

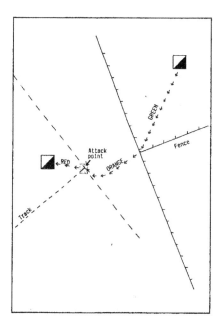

Relocation

When unsure of your position the temptation is to search for the control. However, it is important to relocate by finding a recognizable feature, which can be used as an attack point. Often it is necessary to retrace your steps to a collecting feature that was passed.

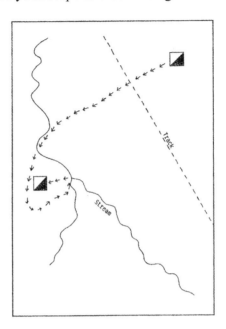

HELPFUL HINTS TO NAVIGATION

Keep the map set (orientated) at all times and move the thumb along the line of travel.

W13B   3.9 km   40 m

1. (51) Between the boulders
2. (66) Ditch end
3. (72) Depression
4. (55) Marsh W.Edge
5. (60) Hill top
6. (55) Stream bend
7. (74) Track junction
Follow streamers to finish

"Between the boulders"   The control will have 51 as the code.

Check the **control description** carefully.

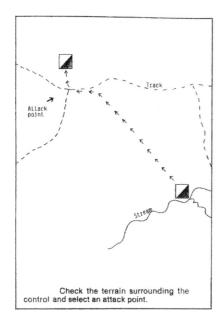

Check the terrain surrounding the control and select an attack point.

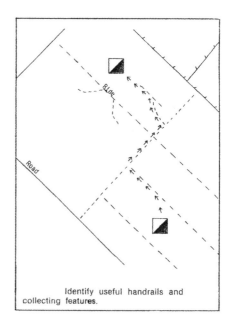

Identify useful handrails and collecting features.

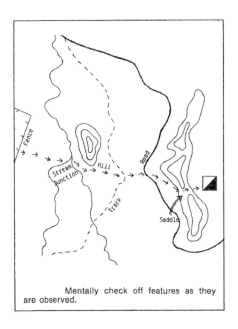

Mentally check off features as they are observed.

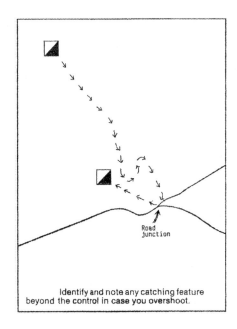

Identify and note any catching feature beyond the control in case you overshoot.

A MAP WALK QUIZ

Use the PRACTICE MAP to help you go through the map walk quiz. Read through the text below and carefully follow the line on the map. Fill in the missing words in the story.

EXERCISE:

At the start we are standing next to the building, with our map oriented and we are looking towards control point 1. We start walking in a (a) _____ direction. Almost at once we pass under some (b)_____. Very soon afterwards we cross a (c)_____. Almost at once we begin to climb a steep hill and come to a (d)_____. We continue this way until we come to a trail. We take the trail until we come to a (e) _____. We have found control 1.

TOWARDS CONTROL 2

After leaving Control 1, we get on a trail going (f)_____. Our route is now fairly level and soon the path brings us to a (g)_____ on our left. Almost immediately we come to a trail junction. We have found Control 2.

TOWARDS CONTROL 3

We follow the trail to the southeast and almost at one we come to another (h)_____. Going to the east we make very slow progress over the next 100 meters because of the (i)_____ we have to scramble over. We soon come to a (j)_____. We have found Control 3.

TOWARDS CONTROL 4

We continue on our way keeping the lake on our right hand side. The lake turns into a marsh, but soon we come to an area to cross. We continue going (k)_____. We have some climbing to do but not much when we come upon a big (l)_____ with a ditch on its eastern border. We have found Control 4.

TOWARDS THE FINISH

We continue traveling south until we come upon a (m) _____. We take the trail to the east until we come to a group of cabins. We have finished our map walk.

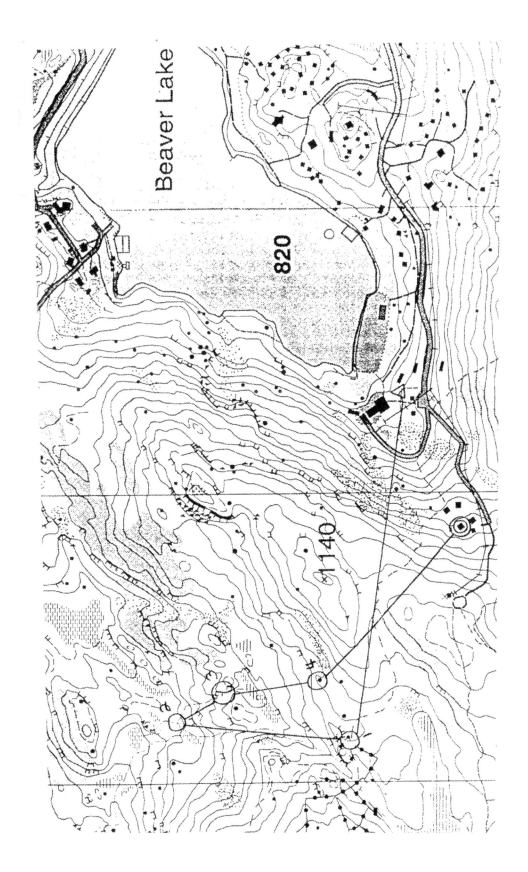

Beaver Lake

820

1140

CHOICE OF ROUTE

During an orienteering race or on a competitive hike, the decision on which route you take from one control to the next is yours alone. You will want to find a quick and economical way, but it also needs to be safe. The route you chose should not leave you too much guess-work in the final stages.

With the help of the map you must try and establish which way is best. You should remember that good trails usually follow valleys and streams, and that a good navigator utilizes 'handrails' as he goes through the terrain, like the edge of a field, power lines or walls, as well as the more obvious guide lines.

In the situation below, you are at control 1 and all set to find control 2. You set the map and study the alternatives. Think, than make your choice. Which is the best route A, B, or C?

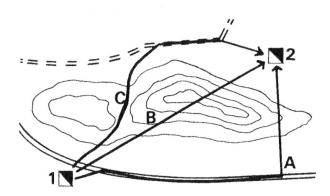

Commentary on the 3 Routes:

A. Fast but very unsafe. It will be difficult to know exactly where to leave the highway. No attack point.

B. Very unsafe and tiring. A tough climb over the hill. Hard to stay on a compass course for such a long session.

C. Obviously the best choice. Quick and safe. The bend in the dirt road will make a fine attack point for the last few hundred feet/meters into control 2.

ROUTE CHOICE EXERCISE

In this exercise you will try to make the best route choice and explain why that is the best way to go. Take into consideration:

CLIMB vs. DETOUR
SHORT HARD ROUTE vs. LONG EASY ROUTE
HANDRAILS and COLLECTING FEATURES

ROUTE CHOICE EXERCISE SHEET	
From 1 to 2 best route is:	From 2 to 3 best route is:
From 3 to 4 best route is:	From 5 to 6 best route is:
From 7 to 8 best route is:	

Explain your choice

1. _____
   _____
   _____
   _____

2. _____
   _____
   _____
   _____

3. _____
   _____
   _____
   _____

4. _____
   _____
   _____

5. _____
   _____
   _____

MAP CHOICE EXERCISE

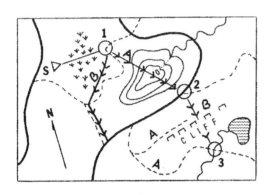

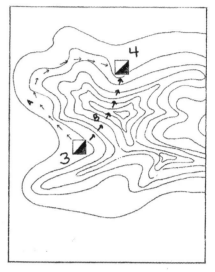

Route Choice from 1 to 2
Route Choice from 2 to 3

Route Choice from 3 to 4

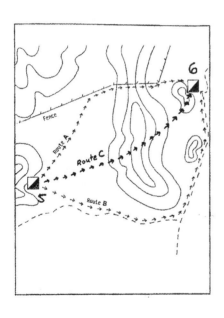

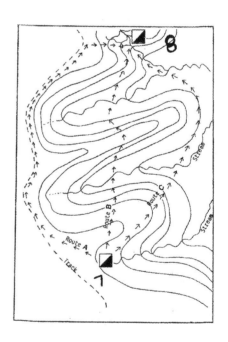

Route Choice from 5 to 6

Route Choice from 7 to 8

SKILL DEVELOPMENT

SETTING THE COURSE

Course lengths should range from one to 2.5 kilometers with 8-12 controls. Remember much of the fun in orienteering is finding the markers.

- Orient the map by terrain in order to read it, and establish the four cardinal directions (N, S, E, and W.)
- Choose a route by using handrails (roads, paths, fences, edges of fields, etc.) in order to establish a safe, reliable, and fast route between controls.
- Use collecting features, (intersecting roads or trails or natural features) which will give you an opportunity to check and see if this is where you think you are.
- Be aware of the basic compass parts. The orienteering compass is used three basic ways:

  1. To orient a map
  2. To measure distance on the map
  3. To establish a direction (bearing) from the map to guide you in following that bearing

- Establish the actual distance between control points and/or key map features. This will involve learning and understanding the metric system, and changing millimeters to meters, etc.
- Establish a pace by counting every second step (double space) between two markers. Try walking and running a distance of 50 meters and repeats it several times to establish a pace.
- Try different variables in pace counting such as going up a hill, down a hill, through the brush, etc.
- Be able to use contour lines to see the difference between hills and valleys and whether or not you are dealing with steep or flat terrain. Contour lines close together reflect steepness and when far apart, flatness.
- Orient the compass. Set the compass to each of the 4 cardinal points and in each case turn the body and the compass to face them. Also take a compass bearing on a landmark. Face a landmark, aim the compass's direction-of-travel arrow at the landmark and orient the compass.
- Test different types of terrain to establish its traverse-ability in terms of:

Climb vs. detour
Short hard route vs. long easy route

- Practice selecting attack points. The presence of a large, distinct, and reliable attack point is often the deciding factor in making your route choice. Find the large attack points first, such as the corner of a field, a path junction, or the bend in a stream, and then with precision compass and pace counting move into the smaller feature.

NAVIGATION TECHNIQUES

QUESTIONS TO ASK BEFORE MOVING

1. What is the feature at the control site?
   Check control description and feature in the center of the circle.

2. What lead me to the control?
   Handrail(s)

3. How will I know I am almost there?
   Attack point

4. How will I know I have gone too far?
   Collecting feature

5. What major features will I see along the route to the control?
   Check off features

6. Fold map to show where you are and just beyond where you are going.

7. Orient map using land features and compass, if necessary.

8. Place thumb on map where you are and move as you reach other major features along your route

At the control site

1. Compare control description code with code on the control flag.
   Punch only if they match.

Repeat the process for each of the controls.

COMPASS ORIENTEERING

Even though orienteering is predominantly a game using maps and sometimes a compass it may become necessary to depend upon the compass solely to figure out where you are. In this activity no maps are used. Each student is given a control card, which indicates bearings of the compass and distances to locate control sites. The participant must use a compass to find control sites. It is important to set the exact bearings on the compass and pace out the distance as indicated. For this activity it is necessary to know the parts of the compass and how to carry and orient a compass. Key factors to consider:

- Always keep the compass level
- Do not try to read the compass around metal objects because this will effect the readings
- Make sure the direction of the travel arrow is pointing straight ahead, in line with the center of the body and waist high
- Turn your body not the compass while holding the compass level and steady until the magnetic needle is lined up in the red box
- Remember to use handrails, attack points and collecting features when trying to locate the control point
- If you can not find the site go back to some recognizable location and try again

Compass bearings are not good for long distances so break the distance down when covering a large distance.

Compass Course

Start at Arch

	DEGREES	DISTANCE (METERS)	CONTROLS
1	320	150	
2	10	100	
3	240	125	
4	140	75	
5	90	75	
6	60	65	
7	90	50	
8	20	160	
9	125	135	
10	200	105	
11	360	50	
12	260	195	

Compass Course

Start at Arch

	DEGREES	DISTANCE (METERS)	CONTROLS
1	320	150	
2	10	100	
3	240	125	
4	140	75	
5	90	75	
6	60	65	
7	90	50	
8	20	160	
9	125	135	
10	200	105	
11	360	50	
12	260	195	

MAKING A SCHOOLYARD MAP

In order to draw a simple sketch map of a schoolyard you will need to do some planning and a little field -work. Careful preparation and attention to detail will take time but is necessary to make a map that is accurate and one that can be used over and over.

Follow these steps to prepare a sketch map of a schoolyard.

Step 1. Equipment
   You will need the following equipment:

- Pencil
- Graph paper
- Compass
- Data chart

Step 2. Determine the scale of your map.
   a. Decide the size of the area to be mapped.
   b. Do this by pacing off the area. Figure out how many paces you take in 10 meters and figure out from there. It doesn't have to work out exactly.
   c. If you use standard paper 8 ½ X 11 a suitable scale for an area 150m X 200m would be 1cm to 10m, which should allow the map area to fit on the paper.

Step 3. Determine what will be included in your map.
   Decide what features (buildings, trees, basketball courts, etc.) you want and choose a symbol to represent each. A typical map legend should appear at the bottom to the map and may look as follows:

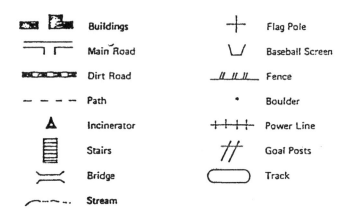

Step 4. Draw Magnetic North.

Draw parallel lines 4cm apart across the paper from the top to bottom and write NORTH at the top.

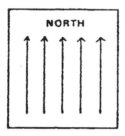

Step 5. Gather Data.
   a. Begin at one corner of the area to be covered by your map. (The corner of the school is a good reliable feature around which to sketch the rest of the map).
   b. From your chosen corner take the bearings on the objects you wish to include in your map. Pace the distance to each object. Record bearing and distance on the data sheet. (See Data Sheet Supplement)
   c. Calculate the map distance using the distances on the data sheet and the scale you selected.

Step 6. Drawing the Map
   It is important to have features located accurately relative to one another.
   a. Begin in the corner of your map that corresponds to the corner from which you took your bearings (building).
   b. Transfer the bearings to the map and measure the proper distance from the corner and draw the proper symbol.
   c. Transfer bearings to map, set compass for bearings given on data sheet. Lay compass on map with base plate touching corner or reference point. Turn entire compass until orienting arrow is lined up with magnetic north line. (Compass base plate should still be against corner and bearing should remain unchanged. Measure the appropriate map distance to put symbol on map.)
   d. Transfer the data from the chart to the map. Measure carefully and recheck bearings with the compass when necessary. Walk from the chosen corner and plot bearings. Measure the appropriate distance in map units and record the symbol on the map.

e. Add the map legend- scale, symbols and direction arrow indicating magnetic north to complete the map.

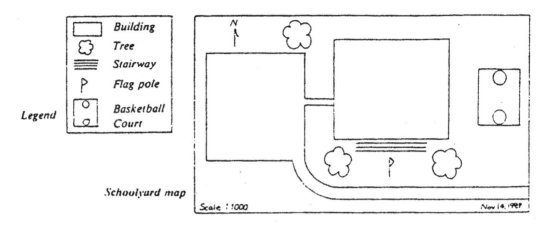

Sample sketch map

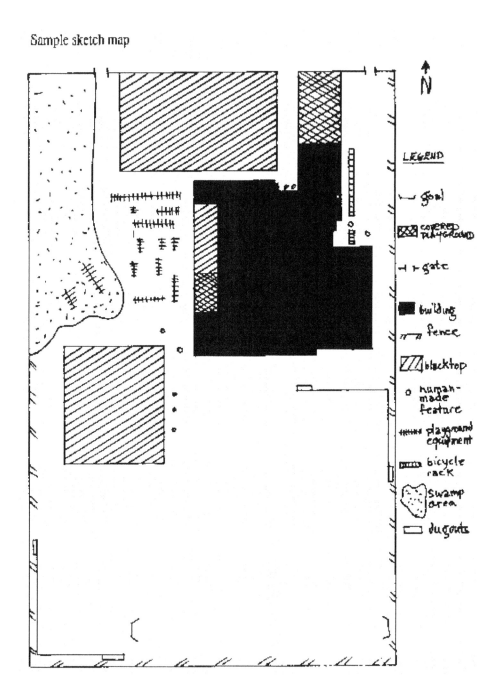

LEGEND

goal

covered playground

gate

building

fence

blacktop

o human-made feature

playground equipment

bicycle rack

swamp area

dugouts

DATA SHEET

Object	Symbol	Bearing	Distance Paces	Map Distance

ORGANIZING & RUNNING A SIMPLE ORIENTEERING MEET

EQUIPMENT

You will need the following:

- A MAP
- CONTROL MARKERS
- PENS, PENCILS, OR PUNCHES
- CONTROL CORDS
- WHISTLE
- WATCH
- COMPASSES

THE MAP

Any map that helps you meet your objectives for the event will do. However, there must be a map. It can be:

- A floor plan of a building, if you are holding the event inside.
- A sketch map of your schoolyard or property.
- A street map with the names of the streets removed.
- A map of a local park.
- A USGS topographic map.

NOTE: Make sure that you have permission to use the area in which you will run your event.

THE CONTROL MARKERS

You need some way of identifying each control site for the participants. A regulation Orienteering marker is an orange and white triangular sleeve made out of nylon or vinyl board. However, you can use your imagination and make markers out of almost anything. Just make sure they are recognizable and not too small.

GLOSSARY

- **Orienting the map** Arranging or holding a map so that the symbols on the map are in the same position as the features they represent on the ground. The map can be oriented either by comparing the map directly with the terrain (orienting by terrain) or by using the compass (orienting by needle).

- **Scale** the relationship between distances on the map to distance on the ground. This information is expressed as a ratio (1:25,000) or as a bar graph on the map.

- **Control** the man-made or natural feature in the landscape upon which a marker is placed, and which is described by a clue.

- **Control marker** Usually a red and white, or orange and white, three dimensional nylon marker used to mark the control location, and equipped with a paper punch and a letter code for orienteering use.

- **Control circles** A circle drawn around a feature on a map to indicate the site at which a control marker is located. The center of the circle is the exact location of the control marker in the terrain.

- **Master map** A map on which the control circles of an orienteering event are drawn and from which each orienteer marks her own map at the start.

- **Folding and thumbing** Fold your map so it shows only the part you need to see at the moment. Use your thumb as a pointer to direct your eye to where you are on the map. This helps you keep on course better and to always know where you are on the map.

- **Handrails** Linear features in the landscape which help to guide you along a route choice. Examples include trails, roads, streams, fences, stone walls, re-entrants, ridges, contour lines, and vegetation boundaries.

- **Collecting features** those natural and man-made features, which we pass enroute to a destination and tell us that we are on course.

- **Catching features** A large feature, usually linear, beyond a destination, which will "catch" or alert us if the destination is passed. May be used as an attack point.

- **Attack Point** A large feature near a destination which can be used to determine one's exact position and from which careful and precise navigation to the destination can be made.

- **Plans of attack** A Plan or organized approach to finding the control, or the attack point.

- **Route choice** the route one selects to follow on the map and in the terrain to a destination.

- **Safety bearing** A compass bearing or direction which will lead directly to a road or a major trail, and which an orienteer can follow to obtain help if lost or injured, or in the event of an emergency.

REFERENCES

Garrett, Mary E. Orienteering and Map Games for Teachers, U.S. Orienteering Federation, 1996.

Gilchrist, Jim, Orienteering—Instructors Manual. Canada: Orienteering. Ontario Publication, 1984.

Hicks, Ed. Orienteering Unlimited, Inc.

Silva Orienteering Services, USA. Teaching Orienteering, Binghamton, NY, 1991.

Wilson, Peter. Orienteering: A Way of Learning Outdoor Navigation, Hillary Commission, 1997.

Nancy Kelly

MATERIALS SUPPLEMENT

MATERIALS SUPPLEMENT

VEGETATION BOUNDARY	PERMANENT BENCH
PERMANENT TABLE	UNCROSSABLE MARSH
POND	CLIFF FACE
CONIFEROUS TREES	DECIDUOUS TREES
TREE STUMP	DRY DITCH
TRAIL/STREAM CROSSING	FENCE CORNER

Nancy Kelly

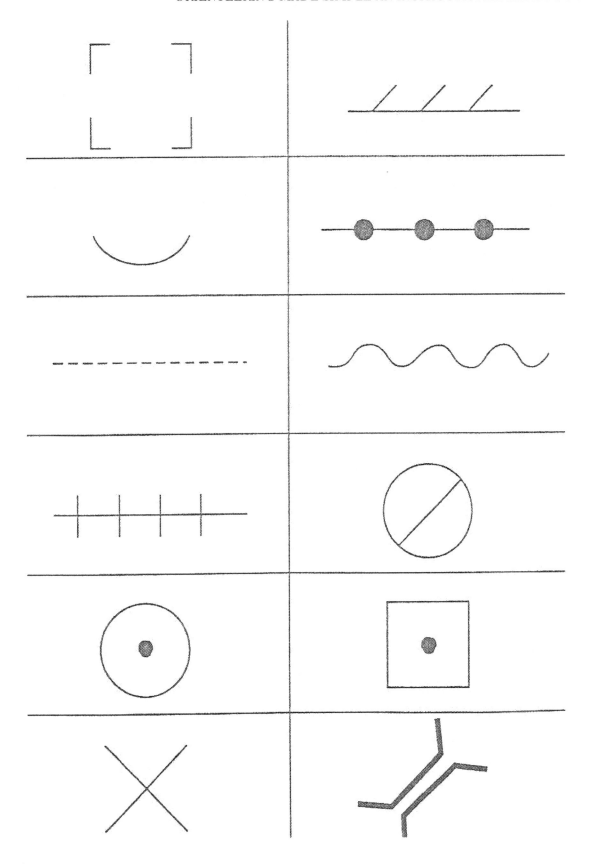

Nancy Kelly

RUIN	FENCE
DEPRESSION	WALL
TRAIL	STREAM
POWERLINE	SEWER
SIGN POST	FLAGPOLE
ROOTSTOCK	BRIDGE

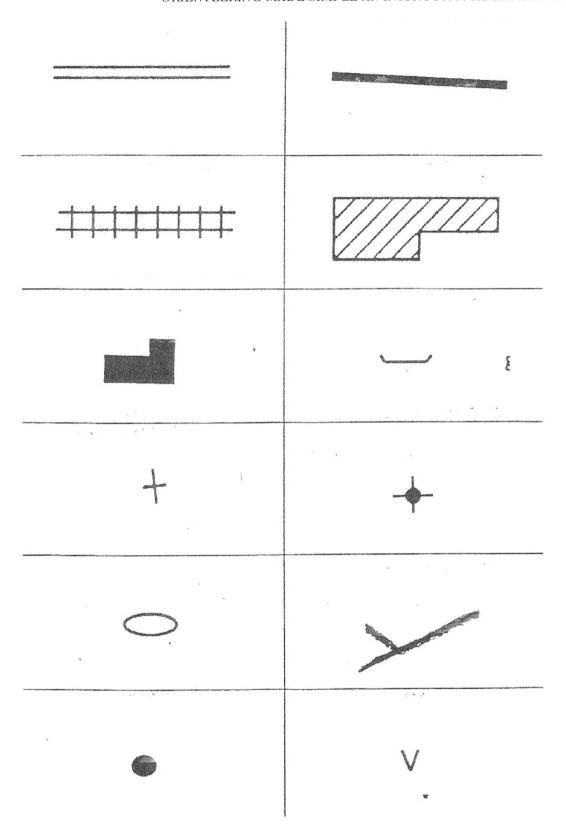

Nancy Kelly

MAIN ROAD	DIRT ROAD
RAILWAY	PARKING LOT
BUILDING	GOAL POST
PLAYGROUND EQUIPMENT	LIGHTPOLE
SMALL HILL (KNOLL)	TRAIL JUNCTION
BOULDER	PIT

CONTROL CARD

1	
2	
3	
4	
5	
6	
7	
8	
9	
10	
11	
12	
13	
14	
15	

CONTROL CARD

1	
2	
3	
4	
5	
6	
7	
8	
9	
10	
11	
12	
13	
14	
15	

Nancy Kelly

MYSTERY "O"

Name: _____   Class Period: _____

SUSPECTS	found	found
Mr. Parker		
Ms. Tisdale		
Mrs. Snow		
Dr. Pipps		
Mr. Brown		
WEAPONS		
Knife		
Revolver		
Tire Wrench		
Rope		
Dumb Bell		
ROOMS		
Library		
Auditorium		
Garage		
Hall		
Lounge		
Study		
Kitchen		
Dining Room		
Court Yard		
Elevator		
Laboratory		

Color Codes

Green	Red	Orange	Purple
Yellow	Blue	Black	Brown

Map Numbers

1	2	3	4
5	6	7	8

Nancy Kelly

TRIVIA ORIENTEERING QUESTION SHEET

#	Trivia Question	Answer
1.		
2.		
3.		
4.		
5.		
6.		
7.		
8.		
9.		
10.		
11.		
12.		

CONTROL CARD

CONTROL CARD

Nancy Kelly

Score Orienteering

Time Limit:15 minutes

Penalty: 5 pts. Per minute late

Control #	Control Letter	Control Value	Control Discription
1			
2			
3			
4			
5			
6			
7			
8			
9			
10			
11			
12			
13			
14			
15			
16			
17			
18			
19			
20			
	Total Points		
	Penalty Pts.	-	
	Final Score	=	

2003 Orientering Made Simple

Nancy Kelly

PRACTICE MAP

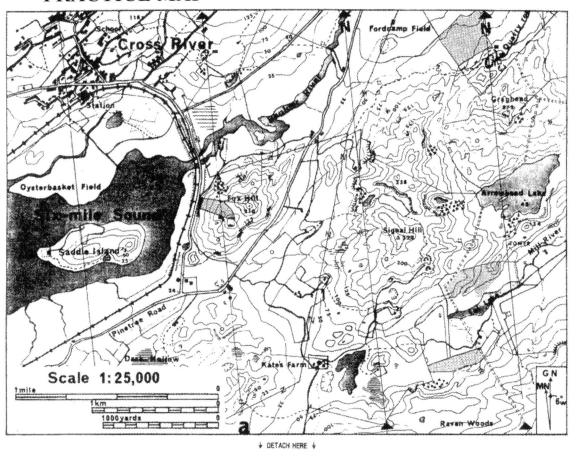

Scale 1:25,000

↓ DETACH HERE ↓

Directions			Degrees	Meters
A	→	B		
B	→	C		
C	→	D		
D	→	E		
E	→	F		
F	→	G		
G	→	H		
H	→	I		
I	→	J		
J	→	K		
K	→	L		
L	→	M		
M	→			
	→			
	→			

Nancy Kelly

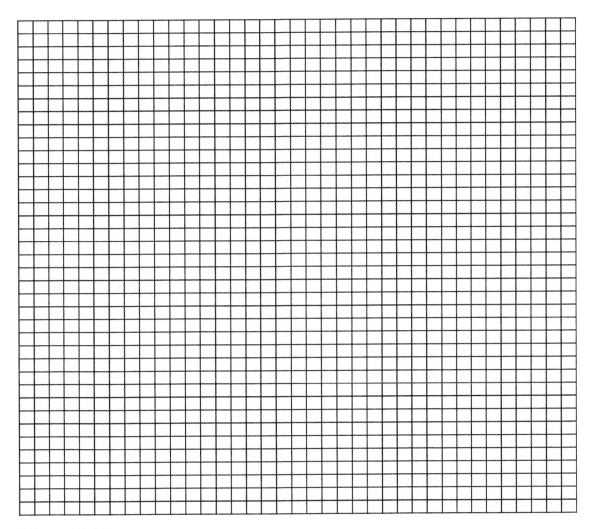

1 Square = 100feet

1	100 North	6	200 W	11	200 SE	16	100 S	21	200 W
2	200 West	7	200 NE	12	300 S	17	200 E	22	400 S
3	200 NE	8	200 E	13	200 E	18	200 SE	23	400 NW
4	200 East	9	300 N	14	200 SE	19	200 W	24	400 SW
5	100 North	10	200 NE	15	200 W	20	110 S	25	400 N

Scale = 1:25,000
        1mm = 25m

Read of bearings to the nearest degree

Directions	Degrees	Meters
S ⟹ 1		
1 ⟹ 2		
2 ⟹ 3		
3 ⟹ 4		
4 ⟹ 5		
5 ⟹ 6		
6 ⟹ F		

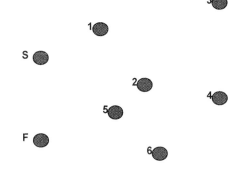

121

ROUTE CHOICE EXERCISE

In this exercise you will try to make the best route choice and explain why that is the best way to go. Take into consideration:

CLIMB vs. DETOUR
SHORT HARD ROUTE vs. LONG EASY ROUTE
HANDRAILS and COLLECTING FEATURES

ROUTE CHOICE EXERCISE SHEET	
From 1 to 2 best route is:	From 2 to 3 best route is:
From 3 to 4 best route is:	From 5 to 6 best route is:
From 7 to 8 best route is:	

Explain your choice

6. _____

7. _____

8. _____

9. _____

10. _____

Nancy Kelly

MAP CHOICE EXERCISE

Route Choice from 1 to 2
Route Choice from 2 to 3

Route Choice from 3 to 4

Route Choice from 5 to 6

Route Choice from 7 to 8

Nancy Kelly

Compass Course

Start at Arch

	DEGREES	DISTANCE (METERS)	CONTROLS
1			
2			
3			
4			
5			
6			
7			
8			
9			
10			
11			
12			

2003 Orienteering Made Simple

Compass Course

Start at Arch

	DEGREES	DISTANCE (METERS)	CONTROLS
1			
2			
3			
4			
5			
6			
7			
8			
9			
10			
11			
12			

2003 Orienteering Made Simple

Nancy Kelly

DATA SHEET

Object	Symbol	Bearing	Distance Paces	Map Distance

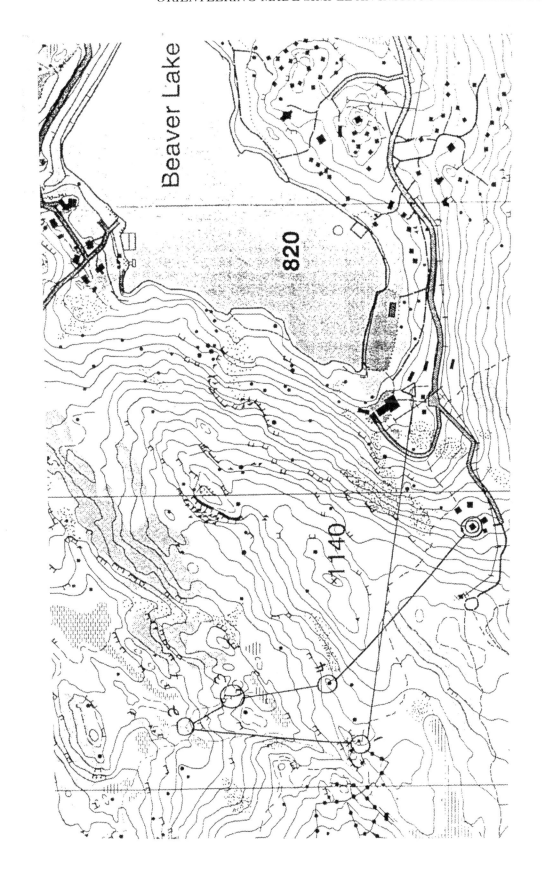

Nancy Kelly

A WALK IN THE WOODS

Once upon a time there were three students who decided to go for a walk in the woods.

They left their ■ and had to cross the ⋯⋅⋅⋅ . They passed many 🌲

and 🌳 as they walked along the ▬▬ .They followed a ⌁

which eventually brought them to a ⟋ . They traveled on the ╌╌╌ which came

to a ➛ . The only way they could get across was by going over a ⋈ . Once they

got to the other side of the ➛ , they came to a ⊶⊶ . They went through and

came upon a ⌐¬ . Inside the ⌐¬ there were ⌐¬ and ⊤

, but they were not in good condition. There were also many large ● which must

have come from the ⌐▯▯▯¬ that was on the North side of the ⌐¬ . They

decided to keep going because it was starting to get dark and there were no ✛

.

They had to climb a ⬯ but at the bottom they came to an ⬭ so they

had to try to go around it. They were beginning to think they would never get out of the

woods when they came upon a ══════ . They saw a ⊙ and they

realized they were almost home.

GOLD CHALLENGE - WRITTEN COMPONENT

Name: _____

COMPASS KNOWLEDGE

Correctly identify 5 compass parts by connecting the term with the part by drawing a line.

1. compass housing

2. direction-of-travel arrow

3. magnetic N needle

4. orienting arrow

5. magnetic north lines

6. measurement scale

Correctly match 5 compass functions.

7. orienting arrow   _____ red end always points magnetic north

8. compass housing   _____ engraved in the housing and runs parallel to north

9. magnetic needle   _____ points to housing's north marking

10. direction-of-travel arrow   _____ rotates to change bearing direction

11. measurement scale   _____ helps with measuring paces on the map

12. orienting lines   _____ followed once the map and compass are oriented

READING A MAP (1)

Study the map of the United States on Sheet 4 and try to answer correctly the following questions.

1. In what state do you live? _____

2. What is the capital of your state?_____

3. What states border your state?_____

4. Which states touch the Gulf of Mexico?_____

5. What ocean is east of the United States?_____

6. What ocean is west of the United States?_____

7. What country is north of the United States?_____

8. Which states touch the Pacific Ocean?_____

9. What state is south of South Dakota?_____

10. What state is north of New Mexico?_____

11. What country is south of Arizona?_____

12. Circle the names of any of the following states which are west of Illinois: California - Pennsylvania - West Virginia - Kansas - Louisiana - Maine Tennessee

13. Circle the names of any of the following states that do <u>not</u> touch the Great Lakes: New York - Indiana - Iowa - Minnesota - Vermont - New Jersey Michigan

READING A MAP (2)

1. New York is located in the: NE, SE, SW, NW

2. Texas is located in the: N, S, E, W

3. Find a four (4) letter state in the west>_____

4. What state is the most NW?_____

5. What state is the most NE?_____

6. What state is the most SE?_____

7. What state is the most SW?_____

8. What state is 40* longitude and 100* latitude?_____

9. What is at 80* latitude and 30* longitude?_____

10. What degree latitude and longitude do you live in?_____

11. What degree latitude and longitude is Nevada? _____

12. How far is it from New York to California? _____

13. How far is it from Delaware to Nebraska? _____

14. If you travel 600 miles west of Iowa where will you be? _____

Nancy Kelly

READING A MAP   (Sheet 4)

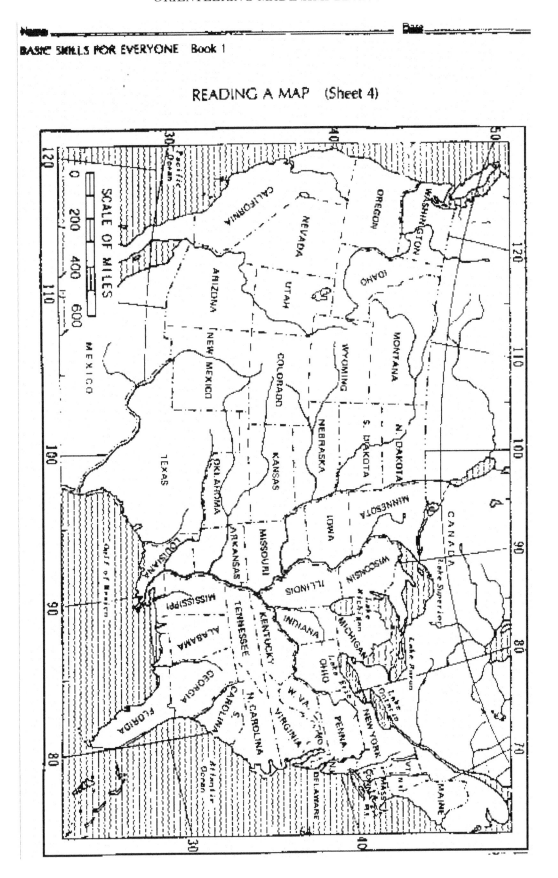

PRACTICE MAP

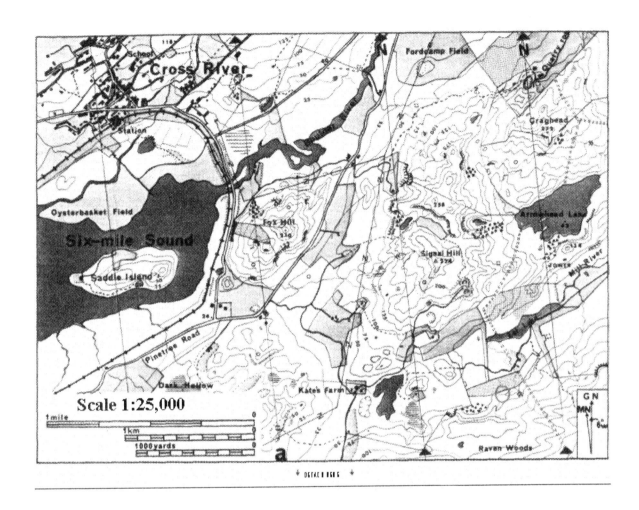

Scale 1:25,000

TRIVIA ORIENTEERING GAME CARDS

Elmer Fudd was always after 'dat' rabbit.	**What two primary colors make purple?**	**What is Chandler's last name on "Friends"?**
Another name for the first day of spring.	**What is Ross's profession on "Friends"?**	**Name the dog on the "Jetsons".**
On "I Love Lucy", who were Lucy and Ricky's landlords?	**The shamrock is the symbol for which country?**	**Give an example of a carbohydrate.**
What is the capital of New Jersey?	**Name the housekeeper and her boyfriend on "The Brady Bunch".**	**The generic name for NaCl is what?**

What does RPM stand for?	The name of the dog on "Beatle Bailey".	What two primary colors make green?
Who is the "Menace" of the comic strips?	Who is Batman's sidekick?	The sons name on the "Jetsons" is what?
Fred Flintstone's next-door neighbor.	Name Donald Duck's three nephews.	What is the capital of New York?
Another name for the first day of winter.	Name the youngest boy and girl on the sitcom "The Brady Bunch".	What is Phoebe's (of "Friends") hit song that was used to market a product?

What river runs through the Grand Canyon?	**Give an example of an oxymoron.**	**Sylvester the cat was always after this bird.**
The boys name on "The Addam's Family".	**Yellowstone National Park is in which state?**	**The chemical symbol for water is what?**

Nancy Kelly

SCORE ORIENTEERING GAME CARDS

A 5	**B** 5
C 5	**D** 5
E 10	**F** 10

J 15	K 15
L 15	M 15
N 20	P 20

Nancy Kelly

R 20	**S** 20
T 20	**W** 20
V 15	**X** 15

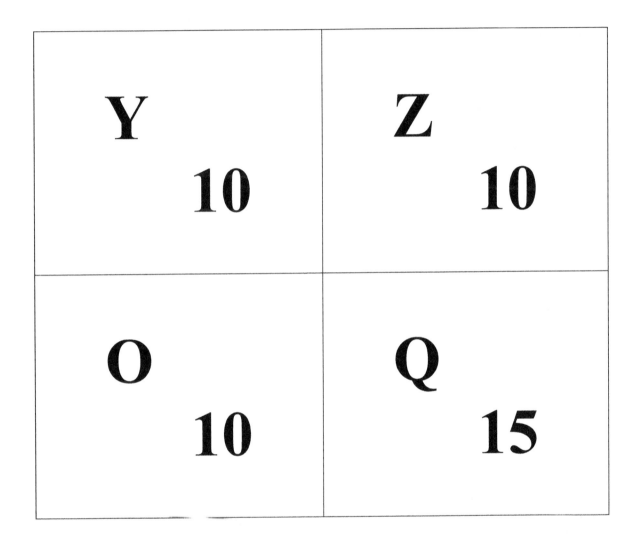

Nancy Kelly

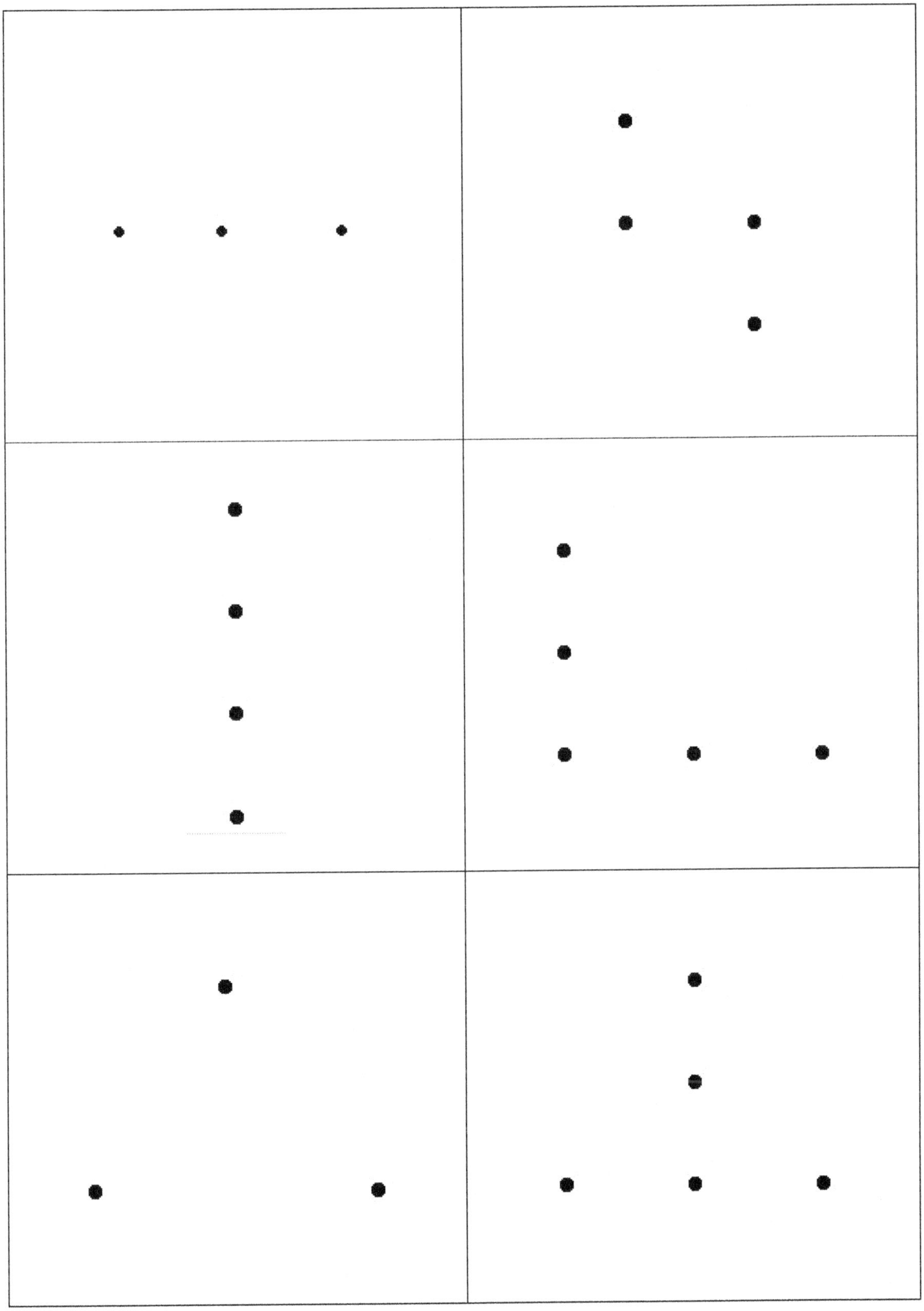

Nancy Kelly

160

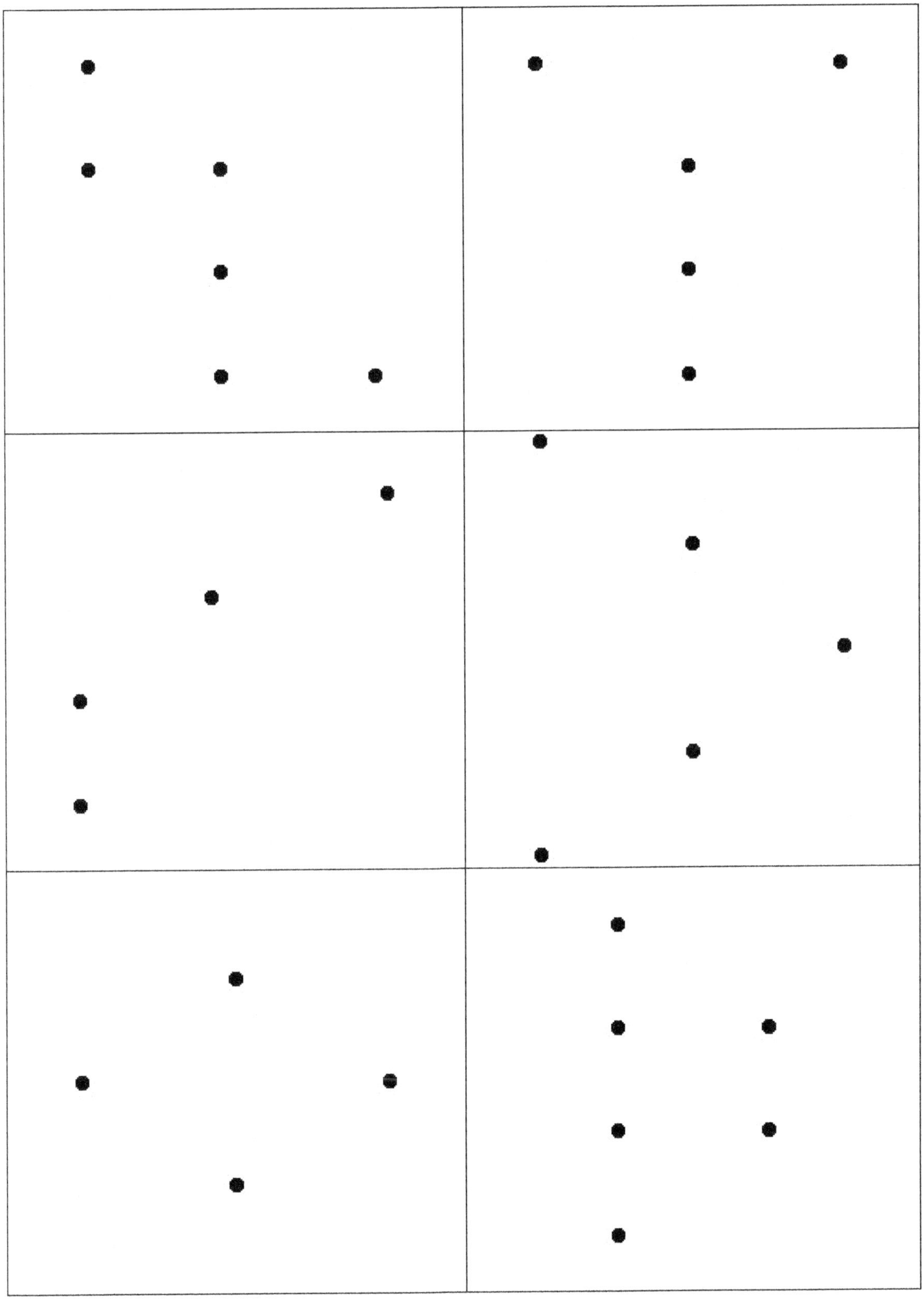

Nancy Kelly

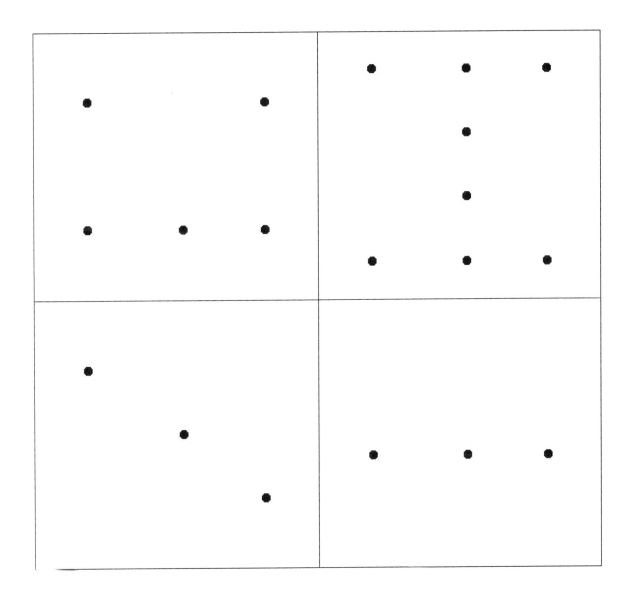

**CONTROL GAME CARDS
(TEAM RELAY, CROSS COUNTRY, COMPASS ORIENTEERING)**

Nancy Kelly

ORIENTEERING ACTIVITY SCHEDULE

1. INTRODUCTION: What is Orienteering? Course Objectives. Types of Orienteering. Holding, Folding, & "Thumbing". ACTIVITY: Draw a Sketch of the Room.

2. STAR ORIENTEERING: "CUNNING RUNNING" (room map & game cards with numbers)

3. POINT TO POINT ORIENTEERING: "THE THINKING SPORT". (room map & game card with numbers)

4. PUZZLE ORIENTEERING (map of school & puzzle pieces)

5. MYSTERY ORIENTEERING: 3 day event (map of school, mystery "O" game cards)

6. MAP SYMBOLS: ROUND-UP

7. MAP SYMBOLS CONTINUED: "A WALK IN THE WOODS" & "MAPPING FANTASY ISLANS". (graph paper)

8. TRIVIA ORIENTEERING (map of front of school & Trivia "O" game cards)

9. PROJECT ORIENTEERING (map of back fields & equipment for projects)

10. SCORE ORIENTEERING (map of entire school grounds & score game cards)

11. TEAM RELAY ORIENTEERING (map of back fields & control cards with dots)

12. CROSS COUNTRY OREINTEERING (map of entire school grounds & control cards with dots)

13. PARTS OF A COMPASS (work sheet & map maze) Activity: "Facing the Cardinal Points" & "Dial-A-Bearing Game.

14. READING A MAP (map of the US & work sheets 1 & 2)

15. STEP COUNTING (teacher copy of step counting activity)

16. SCALE & DISTANCE (teacher copy of sample conversions & PRACTICE MAP)

17. SETTING A MAP (PRACTICE MAP with degrees and meters & Graphing the compass points)

18. SCHOOL-YARD COMPASS GAME (compasses, index cards with bearings, flags with code letters)

19. MAP SKILLS: PUTTING IT ALL TOGETHER:

- Path of Least Resistance
- Contouring
- Using Handrails
- Aiming Off
- Attack Points
- Traffic Lights
- Relocation

ACTIVITY: ROUTE CHOICE EXERCISE & A MAP WALK

20. COMPASS COURSE (Compass Course Game Card) 3 day event

21. MAKING A SCHOOL-YARD MAP (Data Sheet) 3 day event

ABOUT THE AUTHOR

I have been teaching physical education for 17 years and I have written several new programs for the PE curriculum. I like to design creative programs that encourage cooperation, problem solving and decision making. Over the years I have had numerous opportunities to try new programs and make the necessary adjustments or changes in order to make an activity that is fun and challenging. I myself am an avid athlete and I like being active. I am always interested in new challenges and because of this I try to bring this same enthusiasm for adventure to the classroom.

CPSIA information can be obtained
at www.ICGtesting.com
Printed in the USA
BVOW09s0728151116

467884BV00002B/52/P

9 781414 008929